MW00639526

More than **200,000** student reviews on nearly **7,000** schools!

SEE IT ALL ON COLLEGEPROWLER.COM!

This book only offers a glimpse at our extensive coverage of one school out of thousands across the country. Visit *collegeprowler.com* to view our full library of content for FREE! Our site boasts thousands of photos and videos, interactive search tools, more reviews, and expanded content on nearly 7,000 schools.

CONNECT WITH SCHOOLS
Connect with the schools you are most interested in and discover new schools that match your interests.

FIND SCHOLARSHIPS
We give away $2,000 each month and offer personalized matches from a database of more than 3.2 million other scholarships!

SELECT A MAJOR
We have information on every major in the country to help you choose your degree and plan your career.

USE OUR TOOLS TO HELP YOU CHOOSE
Compare schools side-by-side, estimate your chances of admission, and get personalized school recommendations.

*To get started, visit **collegeprowler.com/register***

University of Miami

Coral Gables, FL

Written by Sana Khan, Shawn Wines

Edited by the College Prowler Team

ISBN # 978-1-4274-0640-8

Last updated: 3/24/2011

College Prowler®
5001 Baum Blvd.
Suite 750
Pittsburgh, PA 15213

Phone: (800) 290-2682
Fax: (800) 772-4972
E-Mail: info@collegeprowler.com
Web: www.collegeprowler.com

How this all started...

When I was trying to find the perfect college, I used every resource that was available to me. I went online to visit school Web sites; I talked with my high school guidance counselor; I read book after book; I hired a private counselor. Sure, this was all very helpful, but nothing really told me what life was like at the schools I cared about. These sources weren't giving me enough information to be totally confident in my decision.

In all my research, there were only two ways to get the information I wanted.

The first was to physically visit the campuses and see if things were really how the brochures described them, but this was quite expensive and not always feasible. The second involved a missing ingredient: the students. Actually talking to a few students at those schools gave me a taste of the information that I needed so badly. The problem was that I wanted more but didn't have access to enough people.

In the end, I weighed my options and decided on a school that felt right and had a great academic reputation, but truth be told, the choice was still very much a crapshoot. I had done as much research as any other student, but was I 100 percent positive that I had picked the school of my dreams?

Absolutely not.

My dream in creating College Prowler was to build a resource that people can use with confidence. My own college search experience taught me the importance of gaining true insider insight; that's why the majority of this guide is composed of quotes from actual students. After all, shouldn't you hear about a school from the people who know it best?

I hope you enjoy reading this book as much as we've enjoyed putting it together. Tell me what you think when you get a chance. I'd love to hear your college selection stories.

Luke Skurman
CEO and Co-Founder
luke@collegeprowler.com

Welcome to College Prowler®

When we created College Prowler, we felt it was critical that our content was unbiased and unaffiliated with any college or university. We think it's important that our readers get honest information and a realistic impression of the student opinions on any campus—that's why if any aspect of a particular school is terrible, we (unlike a campus brochure) intend to publish it. While we do keep an eye out for the occasional extremist—the cheerleader or the cynic—we take pride in letting the students tell it like it is. We strive to create a book that's as representative as possible of each particular campus. Our books cover both the good and the bad, and whether the survey responses point to recurring trends or a variation in opinion, these sentiments are directly and proportionally expressed through our guides.

College Prowler guidebooks are in the hands of students throughout the entire process of their creation. Because you can't make student-written guides without the students, we have students at each campus who help write, randomly survey their peers, edit, layout, and perform accuracy checks on every book that we publish. From the very beginning, student writers gather the most up-to-date stats, facts, and inside information on their colleges. They fill each section with student quotes and summarize the findings in editorial reviews. In addition, each school receives a collection of letter grades (A through F) that reflect student opinion and help to represent contentment or satisfaction for each of our 20 specific categories. Just as in grade school, the higher the mark the more content or more satisfied the students are with the particular category.

Each book is the result of endless student contributions, hundreds of pages of research and writing, and countless hours of hard work. All of this has led to the creation of a student information network that stretches across the nation to every school that we cover. It's no easy accomplishment, but it's the reason that our guides are such a great resource.

When reading our books and looking at our grades, keep in mind that every college is different and that the students who make up each school are not uniform—as a result, it is important to assess schools on a case-by-case basis. Because it's impossible to summarize an entire school with a single number or description, each book provides a dialogue, not a decision, that's made up of 20 different topics and hundreds of student quotes. In the end, we hope that this guide will serve as a valuable tool in your college selection process. Enjoy!

The College Prowler Team

Table of Contents

By the Numbers................... **1**

Academics **4**

Local Atmosphere **12**

Health & Safety.................. **19**

Computers.......................... **25**

Facilities............................. **30**

Campus Dining.................. **35**

Off-Campus Dining **43**

Campus Housing **52**

Off-Campus Housing......... **59**

Diversity............................. **63**

Guys & Girls....................... **70**

Athletics............................. **76**

Nightlife............................. **85**

Greek Life **95**

Drug Scene...................... **101**

Campus Strictness **106**

Parking............................. **110**

Transportation **116**

Weather **122**

Report Card Summary ... **126**

Overall Experience **127**

The Inside Scoop............ **131**

Jobs & Internships.......... **140**

Alumni & Post-Grads **142**

Student Organizations.... **145**

The Best **152**

The Worst **153**

Visiting............................. **154**

Words to Know............... **156**

By the Numbers

School Contact

University of Miami
University of Miami
Coral Gables, FL 33124

Control:
Private Non-Profit

Academic Calendar:
Semester

Religious Affiliation:
None

Founded:
1925

Web Site:
www.miami.edu

Main Phone:
(305) 284-2211

Student Body

Full-Time Undergraduates:
9,451

Part-Time Undergraduates:
919

Total Male Undergraduates:
5,484

**Total Female
Undergraduates:**
6,294

Admissions

Acceptance Rate:
44%

Total Applicants:
21,845

Total Acceptances:
9,700

Freshman Enrollment:
2,006

Yield (% of admitted students who enroll):
21%

Transfer Applications Received:
3,572

Transfer Applications Accepted:
1,378

Transfer Students Enrolled:
637

Transfer Application Acceptance Rate:
39%

SAT I or ACT Required?
Either

SAT I Range (25th–75th Percentile):
1740–2050

SAT I Verbal Range (25th–75th Percentile):
570–680

SAT I Math Range (25th–75th Percentile):
600–700

SAT I Writing Range (25th–75th Percentile):
570–670

ACT Composite Range (25th–75th Percentile):
27–31

ACT English Range (25th–75th Percentile):
27–33

ACT Math Range (25th–75th Percentile):
26–32

ACT Writing Range (25th–75th Percentile):
25–30

Top 10% of High School Class:
66%

Application Fee:
$65

Common Application Accepted?
Yes

Admissions Phone:
(305) 284-4323

Admissions E-Mail:
admission@miami.edu

Admissions Web Site:
www6.miami.edu/freshmen/

Early Decision Deadline:
November 1

Early Decision Notification:
December 15

Early Action Deadline:
November 1

Early Action Notification:
February 1

Regular Decision Deadline:
January 15

Regular Decision Notification:
April 15

Must-Reply-By Date:
May 1

Financial Information
Out-of-State Tuition:
$36,188

Room and Board:
$10,800

Books and Supplies:
$2,750

Average Amount of Federal Grant Aid:
$3,114

Percentage of Students Who Received Federal Grant Aid:
18%

Average Amount of Institution Grant Aid:
$16,883

Percentage of Students Who Received Institution Grant Aid:
75%

Average Amount of State Grant Aid:
$6,396

Percentage of Students Who Received State Grant Aid:
44%

Average Amount of Student Loans:
$6,969

Percentage of Students Who Received Student Loans:
44%

Total Need-Based Package:
$29,170

Percentage of Students Who Received Any Aid:
85%

Financial Aid Forms Deadline:
February 1

Financial Aid Phone:
(305) 284-5212

Financial Aid E-Mail:
ofas@miami.edu

Financial Aid Web Site:
www6.miami.edu/ finaidprograms/

Academics

The Lowdown On...
Academics

Degrees Awarded
Bachelor's degree
Certificate
Master's degree
Post-bachelor's certificate
Post-master's certificate

Most Popular Majors
Biology and Biological
Sciences
Business Administration and
Management
Law
Psychology

Majors Offered
Architecture and Planning
Arts
Biological Sciences
Business
Communications
Computer and Sciences
Education
Engineering
Environmental Sciences
Health Care
Languages and Literature
Law
Mathematics & Statistics
Philosophy and Religion

Physical Sciences
Psychology & Counseling
Recreation & Fitness
Social Sciences & Liberal Arts
Social Services

Undergraduate Schools/Divisions

Architecture
Arts and Sciences
Business
Communication
Education
Engineering
Music
Nursing

Full-Time Instructional Faculty

1,001

Part-Time Instructional Faculty

392

Faculty with Terminal Degree

85%

Average Faculty Salary

$90,984

Student-Faculty Ratio

11:1

Class Sizes

Fewer than 20 Students: 52%
20 to 49 Students: 43%
50 or More Students: 5%

Full-Time Retention Rate

90%

Part-Time Retention Rate

64%

Graduation Rate

77%

Remedial Services?

Yes

Academic/Career Counseling?

Yes

Instructional Programs

Occupational: No
Academic: Yes
Continuing Professional: Yes
Recreational/Avocational: No
Adult Basic Remedial: No
Secondary (High School): No

Special Credit Opportunities

Advanced Placement (AP)

Credits: Yes
Dual Credit: Yes
Life Experience Credits: No

Special Study Options

Study abroad
Teacher certification (below
the postsecondary level)
Weekend/evening college

Best Places to Study

Dorm study lounges
Librar
Outside
University Center

Did You Know?

Feel trapped in your dorm room? Many students, equipped with wireless Internet on their laptops, head outside to study by the lake or under a tree.

At the end of every semester, students receive surveys asking them to rank each of their professors in various categories. The results are tallied and posted on the school network to help students select their courses.

Teaching assistants are rare in most courses at UM. Even freshmen lecture classes are almost always taught by full-time faculty members.

Best Places to Study:
library, dorm study lounges, University Center, outside

Students Speak Out On...
Academics

Q Professors

The professors at UM are generally very good compared to other schools. Additionally, because of the (generally) small class sizes, they get to know you on a personal level, and are very willing to work with you.

Q Professors Are Approachaple, Helpful and It Is Easy to Get Individual Attention

One of the best things about UM is the academic life. Despite its reputation, University of Miami students care about their academics and there are always interesting classes to take. Seniors get priority during course registration but there are never any problems getting into classes you need to take for your major. Most classes are smaller than about 25 students, and all of my professors know me by name.

Q History

The department is relatively small and there is not a large variety of courses. However, most professors are extremely good and know what they are talking about.

Q University of Miami Is a Great School

I'm in the College of Arts and Sciences and I am quite pleased with my education. I'm a neurobiology major, and all my professors and advisers are friendly and helpful.

Q Great

The University has an incredible reputation as an academic school and it definitely fulfills it. Most professors are very helpful and they are extremely knowledgeable in their fields. Class sizes are admirable and almost always worth going to class.

Q Academics at UM!

There are variety of majors that are popular at this school, especially marine science, music, business, and communications. My major is Communication Broadcast Journalism. I am a freshman so it was my first time taking classes last semester, and some requirement classes were big and boring. But now it's the second semester, I am taking classes that are smaller and more fun! A lot of classes are based on discussions, and very involving. Classes are tough, but if you study hard then you can get decent grades. If you are struggling academically, then you can always go to free tutoring, or writing center etc. Even though this is not a very small school, professors are nice and very helpful. Studying abroad is a big thing here, and they offer a lot of schools from all over the world. I would really recommend you to join us at the UM :D!

Q The teachers are willing to spend a lot of time with you personally, maybe because this is a private school. Classes are interesting once you get past the intro-level courses, but they're pretty good about AP credits here, so it's easy to AP out of intro level courses.

Q Some classes are interesting, but it really depends on the subject. For example, math classes are boring to me, whereas the science classes are interesting. It really depends on what you prefer as a person.

The College Prowler Take On...
Academics

Back in the 1970s, the University of Miami was known as "Suntan U." Fun-loving hippies flocked from around the country to party on their parents' money for four years. Since that era ended, UM has done a great job in climbing its way into the top tier of American colleges. Although Miami is still a great party town, most of UM's students are here with academics in mind, as well as nightlife and beaches. As a school becomes more prestigious, it builds a strong faculty, and that's exactly what UM has done. Students seem to like their professors, even if they complain regularly about homework and exams. Although complaints about the amount of work and grading are common, it's rare to hear anyone claim that a professor does not know the subject he or she is teaching.

In recent years, the University of Miami has risen its standards of admission considerably. Now more than 40 percent of freshmen were in the top 5 percent of their graduating high school class and two-thirds of all freshmen graduated in the top 10 percent of their high school class. Competition has gotten rigorous. It seems as if every third student at UM is pre-med. Despite this, UM has a long way to go to be able to measure up to the academic tier of Ivy League schools. Nonetheless, Miami is building a great university by combining academics with other aspects of college life. It is safe to say that while the academics are not the toughest in the nation, they are getting there. The professors are mostly good, and there are a few great ones, but overall it feels sometimes as if you are better off reading the textbook than just going to lectures.

The College Prowler® Grade on
Academics: B+

A high Academics grade generally indicates that professors are knowledgeable, accessible, and genuinely interested in their students' welfare. Other determining factors include class size, how well professors communicate, and whether or not classes are engaging.

Local Atmosphere

The Lowdown On...
Local Atmosphere

City, State
Coral Gables, FL

Setting
Suburban

Distances to Nearest Major Cities
Key West – FL – 3 hours, 30 minutes
Orlando – FL – 3 hours, 30 minutes

Points of Interest
American Airlines Arena
Bayside
Coconut Grove
Everglades
Florida Keys
Little Havana
Lowe Art Museum
Metro Zoo
Miami Jai Alai
Nikki Beach
The Oasis
Pro Player Stadium
South Beach
Space

Sunset Place
Ultra
Venetian Pool
Vizcaya Mansion

Shopping Centers
Cocowalk
Dadeland Mall
The Falls
Lincoln Road
Sunset Place
Village of Merrick Park

Major Sports Teams
Florida Marlins: baseball
Florida Panthers: hockey
Miami Dolphins: football
Miami Heat: basketball

Movie Theaters
AMC Cocowalk 16
3015 Grand Ave.
Coconut Grove
(305) 466-0450

AMC Sunset Place 24
5701 Sunset Dr.
South Miami
(305) 466-0450

Bill Cosford Cinema
On campus
(305) 284-4861

Did You Know?

5 Fun Facts about Miami:
• One of Miami's most notable and fun places is its large Cuban neighborhood, known as Little Havana. Head to Calle Ocho (8th Street) to try some great Cuban food and sample other aspects of a fascinating culture.

• Miami's trendy nightlife crowd makes South Beach a hot spot on any night of the week. Keep an eye out for celebrities on the weekends when the clubs get invaded by stars like Will Smith, P. Diddy, and Jennifer Lopez.

• An hour drive south will take you to the start of the Florida Keys, a string of beautiful islands that ends at one of the area's most popular party spots, Key West.

• You never know who you might see walking the streets of Miami. The city was home to at least four recent blockbuster films: Bad Boys II, 2 Fast 2 Furious, Stuck on You, and Out of Time. Countless other music videos and commercials were shot in Miami, as well as films like Scarface and The Birdcage.

• Having a car in college is a great luxury, but make sure to bring plenty of good music, because you could be waiting in traffic for a long time. A 2003 study says the city of Miami has the 4th most congested driving conditions in the country.

Famous People from Miami:
Dave Barry
Jose Canseco
Steve Carlton
Gloria Estefan
Don Francisco
Andy Garcia
Enrique Iglesias
Dwayne Johnson
Catherine Keener
Ricky Martin
Eva Mendes
Chris Myers
Sidney Poitier

Brett Rather
Janet Reno
Alex Rodriguez
Blake Ross
Bob Rubin
Jessica Sutta
Timbaland
Trick Daddy
Vanilla Ice
Persia White

Local Slang:
Laying out – Sprawling out under the sun and getting a tan in one of many of the green spaces on campus
The Grove – Short for "Coconut Grove," a collection of clubs and shops about 10 minutes away from campus
SoBe – Abbreviation for South Beach, home to many of the area's clubs and restaurants
O.B. – Slang term for the Orange Bowl, UM's historic football stadium and former home of the Miami Dolphins

Students Speak Out On...
Local Atmosphere

ℚ GREAT!
There are TONS of things you can do around here at UM. Beaches, pool, shopping...you never get bored.

ℚ Sunset Place/Dadeland Mall
Sunset Place has good places to shop which have realtively good prices while Dadeland Mall is a little bit farther but has palces that sunset doesn't. They oth make it easy to find what you want/need fod school/partying and are good fro scoping out guys/girls ;)

ℚ University of Miami Local Atmosphere
The atmosphere in Miami is incredible. The campus alone is beautiful, along with the town of Coral Gables. There are a lot of places to go to eat and shop. The university of is big on sports and everyone has a lot of school spirit. As for nightlife, there is Coconut Grove and South Beach!

ℚ Can't Beat It
Always something to do

ℚ Lots to Do
There are many restaurants and hangout places nearby campus that will satisfy the need to go out without having to drive all the way to the beach. The metro stops right at campus and there's a university bus which will take you to Sunset Place, a shopping mall just 5 minutes from campus.

ℚ Multicultural Palace
People are friendly. There are malls and events nearby and on the campus.

Q Good Food Location

My school is dead center of many attractions. I can't complain, UNLESS I didnt have a vehicle. Our school buses, (free), take us just about anywhere when there is entertainment there. It just sucks when you don't have a friend with a car too and you want to stay longer... but the buses are shutting it down!

Q

There are a few neighborhoods to avoid, but it's like any other town in America.

The College Prowler Take On...
Local Atmosphere

It's hard not to be impressed by the aura of Miami. Whether it's the authentic Cuban culture in Little Havana or the neon frenzy of South Beach, Miami has plenty to do and see. Sports fans will be impressed by the mixture of professional and collegiate athletics, while entertainment-savvy students will love the music and art scenes. There is definitely not a shortage of things to do, and few cities can match Miami's 24-hour atmosphere. There are things to watch out for, including some bad neighborhoods and insane traffic, but the positives far outweigh the negatives when it comes to Miami's atmosphere.

One of the negatives of having such a great city around the campus is that a "college town" has never been born. Colleges in rural areas usually tend to have small cities spring up around them to accommodate the thousands of students. With so much to do around town, Coral Gables seems to be carrying on daily without thinking too much about the big college next door. Miami is a great city for almost anyone, which is why tourism plays such an important part of the culture. Tourists flock to the beautiful beaches, the endless shops in Coconut Grove, and the clubs and bars of South Beach. Tourists may get a little annoying sometimes, but if you end up going to UM, just remember that you used to be one of them.

B+

The College Prowler® Grade on

A high Local Atmosphere grade indicates that the area surrounding campus is safe and scenic. Other factors include nearby attractions, proximity to other schools, and the town's attitude toward students.

Health & Safety

The Lowdown On...
Health & Safety

Security Office
University of Miami Police Department
5665 Ponce de Leon Blvd., #10
(305) 284-6666
www6.miami.edu/public-safety

Safety Services
Abandoned bicycle confiscation
Alcohol awareness
Anti-theft program
Bicycle lock and registration program
Bicycle safety program
Blue-light phone system
Canes Emergency Response Team (CERT)
Canes Resource Officer program
Closed Door -- Open Floor Q&A sessions
Commuter Watch program
Crime Alert program/ Emergency Notification Network
Crime mapping
Crime stoppers

Crocodile safety program
Custom hands-on programs
Good Behavior reward card
program
Hostile intruder preparedness
program
Identity theft awareness and
prevention program
Laptop larceny program
Library alert program
Operation ID
Pedestrian safety campaign
Personal safety program
Promotional safety items
RAD program
Safe date program
SAFE program
Safety escort services
Sexual assault response team
Stalking/onilne community
safety program
Student crime watch
Student orientation program
Traffic school
Victim advocacy
Video program

Crimes on Campus
Aggravated Assault: 0
Arson: 0
Burglary: 39
Murder/Manslaughter: 0
Robbery: 2
Sex Offenses: 0
Vehicle Theft: 6

Health Center
Student Health Center
5513 Merrick Drive

(305) 284-9100
*www6.miami.edu/student-
health*
Monday–Wednesday 8:30
a.m.-5 p.m., Thursday 9
a.m.-5 p.m., Friday 8:30
a.m.–5 p.m., Sunday 12
p.m.-4 p.m.

Health Services
Allergy injections
Counseling and
psychological services
Immunizations
Lab work
On-site Pharmaceuticals
Pregnancy testing
Primary care
Specialty care/referrals
STD screenings
Travel medicine
Women's health
X-rays

Day Care Services?
Yes

Did You Know?

After 10 p.m., no one is allowed into the residential colleges unless they are a resident or are signed in by a resident.

There are over 70 emergency phones located throughout campus. The phones are easy to spot because of their blue lights. They dial directly to the Department of Public Safety.

The Student Health Center administers flu shots and common immunizations at various times through the year. They'll even come to you, as part of a program that gives flu shots outside all of the dorms at the beginning of flu season every year.

Students Speak Out On...
Health & Safety

Q Police and Safety Services
I feel like the cops really care about the students

Q Safe
I have never had a problem on campus. The security always notifies you by email or other forms of communication if there is any problem, but generally I feel very safe around campus.

Q It's Safe on Campus
There are always patrols on campus so if you are at UM there is no need to worry. But if you are out of campus, you have to be careful.

Q Campus Is Secure
Campus security has really tightened after recent events. Nothing bad happened, but the new emergency warning system in place ensures the safety of everyone on campus. Also, there are blue light security stations and a security officer with a golf cart will come escort you back to your dorm if you don't feel safe at any hour.

Q Security
There has been a lot of things going on campus as far as robberies and shoots (JUST A BB GUN!!!!) but don't let it deter you. The system is better now tha nit was first semester and that is because everyone complained. Now you will get a call, multiple texts emails jsut to keep you notified.

Q Safe

UM is a safe campus. They have their own police department, and they perform well. If there is a security alert though, stay indoors.

Q Lately... I Dont Know

Originally I would've given it an A or so. We recieve e-mails (thankfully) notifying us when a crime or the weather is bad. They tell us to stay in when something has happened on campus or around campus, which is awesome. Over the summer though, there were a couple, if not more, robberies right on campus! I don't know how bad I'd want to work on campus anymore if it is a main target around town. How do these people get in? My school is supposed to be private, maybe we need more security. I will definately feel unsafe this semester at night if I'm walking and there aren't too many people around to hear my scream.

Q Campus=Safe, Surrouding=Not So Much

Campus is beautiful, and you never feel unsafe. The campus police aren't as willing to help you as they make it seems. As safe as you are on campus you must remeber you are in Miami. Campus in a good area of town, but there are some dangerous areas surrounding it.

The College Prowler Take On...
Health & Safety

The majority of students on campus feel safe walking around at night, and there are tons of cops and security guards, as well as emergency phones in case there is ever a problem. Even though Miami can certainly be a dangerous city at times, UM is located in Coral Gables, which is a fairly nice neighborhood. Still, this doesn't hide the fact that several incidences have occurred on campus in recent years. The crimes that were committed, which included burglary and sexual assault, were recognized because of UM's policy of e-mailing the entire student body whenever a serious crime occurs on campus. This is a practice that is not in effect at most of the country's universities. It makes students aware of problems that may exist, though the amount of students outside late at night rarely changes after these alerts.

Although UM officials are very concerned with crime on campus and they heavily investigate any threats, it's important for students to know that crime is, at times, an issue. The Department of Public Safety should be commended for its honesty about what's happening around campus. The department's truthfulness in these matters makes students feel more comfortable walking around at night. No matter how many police officers the school hires there will always be a risk. The most important thing is that an overwhelming majority of students feel safe on campus and that there is very little threat of extremely serious crimes.

The College Prowler® Grade on

Health & Safety: C+

A high grade in Health & Safety means that students generally feel safe, campus police are visible, blue-light phones and escort services are readily available, and safety precautions are not overly necessary.

Computers

The Lowdown On...
Computers

Wireless Access
Yes: Campus-wide

24-Hour Labs?
Yes: Only during exams

Charged to Print?
Yes: $100 free, then 5-cents a page for black and white or 10-cents a page for color

Special Software & Hardware Discounts
None

Did You Know?

The school library alone contains 128 computers with Internet access and free printing to every one in 10 printers.

Every residential college on campus has a computer lab in its lobby.

Students Speak Out On...
Computers

Wireless Access
Wireless access to the Internet is available all over the campus. The signal is very strong all over the campus.

Everything Is Great
Computers on campus are great. Most are PCs but some are Macs and all are connected to printers in the general area. Printing is really easy and great. The entire campus has WIFI and that is a big plus!

Richter Computer Lab
The Coral Gables on-campus library has about 100 computers, and they are filled most of the time (especially around mid-terms and finals). Each dorm also has a small computer lab; I find that there tend to be more computers available there. The one problem with their labs is that they now give you a $100 stipend for printing paper (at 5 cents a page), so if you have a paper intensive class I suggest you get a printer. They started this new policy last year. The printers don't always work, either. The campus has great WiFi, included in your tuition. They also have an IT office that sets everything up for you on your PC or laptop, including Microsoft XP/Vista, wireless/cable, and Microsoft Office. This is also included in your tuition.

Wireless Access
The wireless access is very efficient. Anyone can get access to the internet on the school campus. The internet is fast. However, if you live on one of the top floors of the dorms, it is slow.

Q Computers

wireless access can be spotty at times. Computers in library however work perfectly fine.

Q Network/Wireless

The network is usually pretty good in the towers, although if you are going to live on anything above the 5th floor, it would be best to get an cable just in case. Sometimes the network picks up and the gets lost but you get used to it.

Q Would Be Great If Not for the Inconsistency

The WiFi in the dorms is very inconsistent. The Mac Computers in the music library are great but rarely are able to get online. Richter library computers are fast, but they are PC only at this time. WiFi across campus is unreliable. Students are barred from using Torrent sites or rapidshare style sites. Printing on campus is a hassle.

Q The computers are good, except in the library; you sometimes have to wait forever to get a turn using them during the day.

The College Prowler Take On...
Computers

Movies like Terminator and The Matrix predict that computers will someday take over earth and enslave the human race. What better reason could there be for keeping one in your dorm room? Having a computer in college is more of a social luxury than an academic necessity. Computer labs can be found in the lobby of every UM residence hall, as well as the library, and they're hardly ever full. It's much more convenient, however, to lay in bed like a lazy walrus with a laptop and finish your homework that way. Those who can afford it should bring a computer to college. A laptop with a long cord is a plus, because then, if you have a fridge close by and a strong bladder, there will be no reason to ever get out of bed on the weekends.

Like most colleges, UM has a fast and fairly reliable network that gives you easy access to the Internet, and the campus-wide wireless network is a huge asset if you have a laptop. The system does go down occasionally, but it almost always comes back within a few minutes. For students looking to cut back on spending, rest assured that you can complete your assignments in the computer labs. They stay open late—some past midnight—and always have a staff member there to help with technical problems. But the majority of students who use the labs are only there to fulfill the requirements of archaic professors who still want assignments saved on floppy disks, a feature left off many modern computers.

The College Prowler® Grade on
Computers: B+

A high grade in Computers designates that computer labs are available, the computer network is easily accessible, and the campus's computing technology is up-to-date.

Facilities

The Lowdown On...
Facilities

Campus Size
260 acres

Student Centers
The Whitten University
Center (UC)

Main Libraries
12

**Service & Maintenance
Staff**
197

Popular Places to Chill
The Rat
The Rock
Storm Surge Cafe
The UC
UC Patio

Bar on Campus
The Rathskellar

Bowling on Campus
None

Coffeehouse on Campus
Hurricane Food Court
The Coffee Company

Movie Theater on Campus
Bill Cosford Cinema in the Memorial Building

Favorite Things To Do
Some students gather in the Storm Surge Café at the UC
to play pool, table tennis, foosball, backgammon, chess,
and checkers, or watch TV. This area is open Monday-Friday
9 a.m.-11:30 p.m. and Saturday-Sunday 11 a.m.-11:30
p.m.Others enjoy working out at the Wellness Center or
playing sports on the massive IM Fields. Of course, there are
also numerous Division 1A sporting events on and off campus,
all of which are free to UM students with their ID cards.
The Wellness Center is a state-of-the-art gym located near two
of the residential colleges. Access is free to students, making
it a great place for health-conscious students and those just
looking to play some basketball or take a swim. There are also
free movies for students at the campus theater, comedians
and musicians at the Rathskellar, and top touring bands at
the Convocation Center, which doubles as a basketball arena.
Every Thursday from 12 p.m. to 1:30 pm a different band
performs live on the UC Patio. This event is a free music series
that showcases local, regional and national bands. There is
always some event being outside by the Whitten University
Center, too, and the Bank United Center on the Coral Gables
campus hosts concerts, family shows, trade shows, lectures,
and sporting events. During the 2008 election season,
President Obama held a rally at the Bank United Center.

Students Speak Out On...
Facilities

Q The Library Is Always Reliable
At the University of Miami, one can always count on the library. For one's addictive Facebook cravings or last minute cramming sessions, the library is always open for its culturally diverse student body. There are always aids available in case of those awful last minute printer jams or difficult book searches. This library is as reliable as this website.

Q Law School Library
The best library oncampus. Richter is nice but wayy to noisy at times. The law school just has a different vibe with it it is comforting instead of creepy.

Q Computer Labs Are Great.
Computer labs are great. The computer labs are top of the line and easily accessible. They are always open and manned by school personal who are always ready to help and give advise. Labs are set up so you have complete privacy or a group of people can work on a project together. The labs are open until late so students can work at anytime.

Q Great!
Athletic Center is awesome! it has everything! including massage places, racket ball, yoga studios... Library is good as well. There are lots of campus activities. So many clubs. Campus is beautiful.

Q Campus Facilities
There is so much to do on the U Miami campus. The gym is open until midnight with an assortment of work out

supplies, the on campus store is open nearly 24 hours a day with everything you will need for late night studying, and there is so much help offered in the libraries and computer labs. The art exhibits are beautiful and diverse as well.

Q UC Is Okay

The University Center gets pretty busy during the day but is dead when classes aren't in session. There's a convenient food court, a nice outdoor patio, and a pool that's open year round. However, it's an older building that could use a few upgrades. It's great during the day though to go relax, meet up with friends, grab a bite to eat, or get a tan.

Q Leto High School

The facilities at my school are quite clean and provide a good learning environment for students. Our library is open all day during school ours with a substantial amount of computers available for students to research. The school has a variety of clubs to choose from each with their own individual aspect of any type of subject.

Q

The facilities, which span all interests, are all top-notch. The Wellness Center has top-of-the-line sporting amenities for any activity one may seek to pursue. The bookstore, University Center, and dining halls are all clean and technologically sound.

The College Prowler Take On...
Facilities

Although most of the classroom buildings around UM are hideously ugly, the insides are generally decent and the newer buildings are very nice. The highlight of UM's facilities is, by far, the Wellness Center—a huge gym located next to the dorms where most freshmen live. The building stays open until midnight on weeknights, allowing for late-night games of basketball, squash, or racquetball, which can provide a great study break. The multi-level gym has pretty much anything a student could want, and this is definitely something to look forward to when coming to UM. The other place where students spend a lot of time is the University Center, aptly located in the center of campus. The UC has a lounge with televisions, an information desk, food court, offices, and a convenience store, and it's attached to the bookstore and campus post office.

The UC is a nice enough place and will most likely only improve. There is a movie theater in a corner of campus that shows relatively new movies free to students, as well as art-house fare. Construction is booming on all of UM's campuses, from a new nursing school facility, lecture and gallery spaces at the School of Architecture, a music library and technology center, and student center for the School of Communication on its Coral Gables campus, to a 15-story Clinical Research Institute and Wellness Center at its medical school.

The College Prowler® Grade on

A high Facilities grade indicates that the campus is aesthetically pleasing and well-maintained; facilities are state-of-the-art, and libraries are exceptional. Other determining factors include the quality of both athletic and student centers and an abundance of things to do on campus.

Campus Dining

The Lowdown On...
Campus Dining

Meal Plan Available?
Yes

24-Hour Dining
None

Average Meal Plan Cost
$4478 per year

Average Meals/Week
20

Freshman Meal Plan Required?
Yes

Dining Halls & Campus Restaurants

Convenience Store

Location: University Village
Food: Snacks
Hours: Monday-Thursday
8 a.m.-10 p.m., Friday
8 a.m.-11 p.m.,
Saturday-Sunday 11 a.m.-11 p.m.

Convenience Store

Location: UC
Food: Snacks
Hours: Monday–Thursday 7 a.m.–2 a.m., Friday 7 a.m.-4 a.m., Saturday 9 a.m.–4 a.m., Sunday 9 a.m.-2 a.m.

Jamba Juice

Location: Hurricane Food Court
Food: Smoothies
Hours: Monday–Thursday 8:30 a.m.–7 p.m., Friday 8:30 a.m.–4 p.m.

Jenkins Snack Bar

Location: Jenkins School of Business
Food: Snacks
Hours: Monday-Thursday 7:30 a.m.-7:30 p.m., Friday 7:30 a.m.-5 p.m.

Mahoney/Pearson Dining Hall

Location: Next to Mahoney/ Pearson Residential College
Food: Buffet-style options
Hours: Monday–Thursday 7 a.m.–9 p.m., Friday 7 a.m.–7 p.m., Saturday 9 a.m.–7 p.m., Sunday 11 a.m.–7:30 p.m.

Mango & Manny's Market Place

Location: Hurricane Food Court
Food: Caribbean
Hours: Monday-Thursday 8 a.m.-5 p.m., Friday 8 a.m.-4 p.m.

Market Square

Location: Hurricane Food Court
Food: Salad bar, soups
Hours: Monday–Friday 11 a.m.–4 p.m.

Nikos

Location: Hurricane Food Court
Food: Mediterranean
Hours: Monday-Thursday 11 a.m.-6 p.m., Friday 11 a.m.-4 p.m.

The Oasis

Location: UC
Food: Kosher deli
Hours: Monday-Thursday 8 a.m.-7 p.m., Friday 8 a.m.-3 p.m.

Olo Sushi

Location: Hurricane Food Court
Food: Sushi
Hours: Monday-Thursday 10 a.m.-5 p.m., Friday 10 a.m.-4 p.m.

Panda Express

Location: Hurricane Food Court
Food: Chinese
Hours: Monday–Thursday 11 a.m.-6 p.m., Friday 11 a.m.-4 p.m.

Salsarita's

Location: Hurricane Food Court
Food: Mexican
Hours: Monday-Thursday 10:30 a.m.-7 p.m., Friday 10:30 a.m.-4 p.m.

Satellite Carts

Location: Various walkways and courtyards around campus
Food: Chips, cookies, soda, and other snacks for between classes
Hours: Monday–Friday 8 a.m.–2 p.m.

Sbarro

Location: UC
Food: Pizza/Italian
Hours: Daily 11 a.m.-12 a.m.

Stanford Dining Hall

Location: Next to Stanford Residential College
Food: Buffet
Hours: Monday–Thursday 7 a.m.–9 p.m., Friday 7 a.m.–7 p.m., Saturday 9 a.m.–7 p.m., Sunday 11 a.m.–7:30 p.m.

Starbucks

Location: Near Richter Library
Food: Coffee, pastries
Hours: Monday-Thursday 7 a.m.-11 p.m., Friday 7 a.m.-8 p.m., Saturday 9 a.m.-5 p.m., Sunday 10 a.m.-9 p.m.

Subway

Location: Law School
Food: Sandwiches, salads
Hours: Monday–Thursday 7 a.m.-12 a.m., Friday 7 a.m.-10 p.m., Saturday 10 a.m.–8 p.m., Sunday 11 a.m.-8 p.m.

Wellnes Center Juice Bar

Location: Wellness Center
Food: Energy drinks, juice, smoothies, protein bars
Hours: Monday–Thursday 7:30 a.m.-10 p.m., Friday 7:30 a.m.-7 p.m., Saturday-Sunday 11 a.m.-5 p.m.

Wendy's

Location: Hurricane Food Court
Food: Fast food
Hours: Monday-Thursday 10 a.m.-10 p.m., Friday 10 a.m.-6 p.m.

Student Favorites

Mango & Manny's Market
Place
Nikos
Wendy's

Special Options

Most of the places in the
food court are only open for
lunch, but Sbarro, Subway,
and the Rat are usually open
later.

Did You Know?

The dining halls stay open late once per semester for a "midnight breakfast" to help students who are up late studying for finals.

The dining halls are stocked with current issues of the student newspaper, as well as free copies of the local papers and USA Today for students to read while eating.

Students Speak Out On...
Campus Dining

Q Very Good
Dining options are very good, there is a good amount of things to choose from.

Q Food Court
I am a commuter so only eat at the food court not at the dining hall and there is a lot of variety there.

Q OK I Guess
Not my cup of tea but better than what I get on the streets.

Q They're Great but Pricy
I guess I couldn't ask for something less considering the school choice. The meal plans are great, and we have a wide selection in our cafeteria. If you want to go off campus there is also a TGIF that stays open until 2am just for our school right across the street.

Q Foods and Dinning Not the Greatest
If you live in a dorm you are require to eat at the cafateria, but for a student, like me, eats around places on campus. I live in the school apartment and don't have to eat in school. In my apartment I cook because our school provied expensive food that are not the greatest. Also foods, such as Wendeys, which it is horrible for my health. To conclude, the food and the dinning center is just fine, but I have not eaten the food very often.

Q Bland
There is some variety, but it's very bland and repetitive for the most part. It falls short of other schools dining options

Q Standard Minus One Aspect

Dining hall food is run-of-the-mill dining hall food. Not too good so you'll end up finding something you can bare/enjoy a little bit and you'll eat it way too much.Meal plans for dining halls are strict. Other people can't swipe for you. It's 8.50 or 9 bucks for a meal at the dining hall so if you run out, you're out of luck. Not much versatility in meal plan. If you're a freshman you can get 14 or you can get 20. 14 is not enough for some people and 20 is too many for nearly 99% of the students.Food Court, C-store, Sbarro's, and Subway are all pretty good options. You get 50$ to spend at these places for the semester when you get the 20 meal plan. You get $150 when you get the 14 meal plan. Food court, C-store, and Sbarro's are located in the middle of campus and are easy to get to.The problem is that on weekends, the food court closes. It also has terrible hours. Most places close before 5pm so dinner is limited to the dining hall, Sbarro's, or Subway.

Q

Dining halls are dining halls, anywhere you go. The food court is great, and the Rathskellar, also known as the Rat, is a great place to chill in between classes and shoot some pool.

The College Prowler Take On...
Campus Dining

The school has two dining halls, both with pretty standard college buffet food. The variety sounds good—pizza, pastas, made-to-order sandwiches, hamburgers, hot dogs, fries, salads, and ice cream are only a few of the daily staples—but nothing is of very high quality. Most students don't mind the food at first, but they get really sick of it sometime around Halloween of their freshman year. This is about how long it takes to realize that all the different foods have the same greasy taste. Even the salad and the ice cream are almost indistinguishable if you don't look at them.

Freshmen usually start with the comfortable 14-meal plan, which allows for 14 meals at the dining hall per week. Unless you were raised on Sizzler, you'll probably drop that to the eight-meal plan for your second semester, which is the minimum UM allows for a student living on campus. Either plan gives the student "dining dollars" that can be used like a debit card at the restaurants on campus. The 14-meal plan comes with $150 in dining dollars per semester, and the eight-meal plan gets you $200. This money is pretty valuable since UM has an excellent selection of fast food restaurants on campus. There's a food court with Nikos, Panda Express, Jamba Juice, and Starbucks, and there's even an overpriced take-out sushi bar if you feel like blowing all your dining dollars on the first day. Other places to eat include Sbarro, Subway, and the Rathskeller, a sports bar and popular meeting place. If you don't use all of your dining dollars by the end of the semester, you can always head over to the campus convenience store and spend the remainder on junk food and prehistoric donuts.

B

The College Prowler® Grade on

Campus Dining: B

The grade on Campus Dining addresses the quality of both school-owned dining halls and independent on-campus restaurants as well as the price, availability, and variety of food.

Off-Campus Dining

The Lowdown On...
Off-Campus Dining

Restaurant Listings
Bangkok Bangkok II
Food: Thai
157 Giralda Ave., Coral
Gables
(305) 444-2397
www.bangkokbangkok.net
Price: $8-$15
Cool Features: The décor
at Bangkok Bangkok is
fabulous! The low tables
and pillows to sit on give
the place a very authentic
feel. There is another area
for those who want to sit in a
regular restaurant setting.

Casola's
Food: Italian
2437 SW 17th Ave., Miami
(305) 858-0090
Price: $5-$10
Cool Features: Massive slices
of pizza available for delivery

The Cheesecake Factory
Food: American
7497 Dadeland Mall, South
Miami/Kendall

(305) 665-6400
www.thecheesecakefactory.com
Price: $10-$20
Cool Features: Order dessert from a long list of flavored cheesecakes

Chicken Kitchen
Food: Spanish, Cuban, fast food
7315 Red Road, South Miami
(305) 669-0099
www.chickenkitchen.com
Price: $5-$10
Cool Features: Serves traditional chicken–style dishes

Denny's
Food: American
1150 S. Dixie Hwy.
(305) 666-6250
www.dennys.com
Price: $8-$15
Cool Features: The only 24–hour dining within walking distance of campus.

Havana Harry's
Food: Cuban/Spanish
4612 S. LeJeune Rd.
(305) 661-2622
Price: $10-$20

Hooters
Food: Sandwiches, hamburgers, seafood, wings
3015 Grand Ave., Suite 330

(305) 442-6004
www.hooters.com
Price: $8-$15

House of India
Food: Indian
22 Merrick Way, Coral Gables
(305) 444-2348
Price: $10-$30
Cool Features: Wonderful food and great service!

Jerry's Famous Deli
Food: Sandwiches/deli
1450 Collins Ave., Miami Beach
(305) 532-8030
www.jerrysfamousdeli.com
Price: $8-$15

Johnny Rockets
Food: American
5701 Sunset Dr., Sunset Place
(305) 663-1004
www.johnnyrockets.com
Price: $5-$10
Cool Features: Throwback to the '50s craze of burgers, fries, and shakes.

Kendall Ale House
Food: Seafood bar and grill
11625 N. Kendall Dr.
(305) 595-7448
Price: $10-$20
Cool Features: 1 mile from Amerisuites hotel

La Carreta
Food: Cuban
3632 SW Eighth St., Calle Ocho

(305) 444-7501
www.lacarreta.com
Price: $5-$10
Cool Features: It's like taking
a trip to Cuba!

Los Ranchos
Food: Steakhouse
3015 Grand Ave., Coconut
Grove
(305) 461-8222
www.beststeakinmiami.com
Price: $15-$30
Cool Features: Known for
its Churrasco, which is a
tenderloin steak that is
topped with Chimichurri.
There are ethnic musical
performances on the
weekends.

Miami's Best Pizza
Food: Italian
1514 S. Dixie Hwy., Coral
Gables
(305) 666-5931
www.miamisbestpizza.com
Price: $5-$10
Cool Features: Offers delivery

Riviera Pizza
Food: Italian
1558 S. Dixie Hwy.
(305) 666-3730
Price: $3-$8
Cool Features: Special pizza
deal for UM students; also
delivers

Sunset Tavern
Food: American
7232 SW 59th Ave., South
Miami
(305) 665-9996
www.delilane.com/sunset.
php
Price: $5-$10

Swensen's Ice Cream Parlor
& Restaurant
Food: American/ice cream
1586 S. Dixie Hwy.
(305) 661-7658
swensensrestaurant.com
Price: $5-$10
Cool Features: Famous for
old–fashioned ice cream
sundaes

Texas Taco Factory
Food: Mexican
475 S. Dixie Hwy., Coral
Gables
(305) 662-2212
Price: $5-$10
Cool Features: Delivery,
drive–thru, and dining room.

TGI Friday's
Food: American
1200 S. Dixie Hwy., Coral
Gables
(305) 668-7808
www.tgifridays.com
Price: $8-$15
Cool Features: Watch live
sports games in the bar area

Versailles Restaurant

Food: Cuban

3555 SW Eighth St., Calle Ocho

(305) 445-7614

Price: $5-$10

Cool Features: Cuban specialties in a casual family style atmosphere

Wild Oats Natural Marketplace

Food: Organic cheeses, fair trade coffee, wine, full–service meat and fresh seafood

11701 S. Dixie Hwy., Pinecrest

(305) 971-0090

Price: $5-$10

Cool Features: Natural and organic products

Best Breakfast

Denny's

Jerry's Famous Deli

Best Healthy

Pinecrest Wild Oats
Marktplace

Best Pizza

Casola's

Miami's

Riviera Pizza

Best Wings

Hooters

Kendall Ale House

Best Place to Take Your Parents

Cheesecake Factory

Havana Harry's

Los Ranchos

24-Hour Dining

Denny's

Jerry's Famous Deli

La Carreta

McDonalds

Taco Bell

Other Places to Check Out

Lotus Garden

Outback Steakhouse

Grocery Stores

Publix

1401 Monza Ave., Coral
Gables

(305) 667-1681

Whole Foods

6701 Red Road, Coral Gables

(305) 421-9421

www.wholefoods.com

Winn–Dixie

5850 SW 73rd St., South
Miami

(305) 666-5241

Did You Know?

Some of the best bars around Miami also double as trendy restaurants during the day and early evening.

For a massive selection of late-night dining, take a 20-minute drive over the bridge to South Beach, where nothing closes early.

Every spring, celebrity chefs flock to Miami for the South Beach Wine & Food Festival. Past guests have included Food Network favorites Emeril Lagasse and Bobby Flay.

Students Speak Out On...
Off-Campus Dining

Q The Strip to the Grove

All along the two mile or so stretch from the university to the grove, a rich variety of restaurants can be found. These range from your neighborhood pizza and burger shops to fancy bbq restaurants and asian cuisines. Once your reach the grove you find a melting pot of different cultures that is able to satisfy any individuals dining desires; with prices that vary from well within a college students budget to prices that will clear out your wallet before you can blink!

Q Beyond American Dinning

Off campus eating at Miami is unique. Anything you desire is acquirable. If you want to fall in love, get your mind blown, visit another country, or just enjoy yourself. All you have to do is search the areas around the university and go to the best restaurants in all of Florida. The serving is incredible, food is exquisite, and the atmosphere is life awakening

Q Off-Camus Dining

Several restaurants, conveniently located within walking distance, just across US1, strive on student consumers. These include Denny's, TGI Friday's, Moon Japanies and Thi, Miami's Best Pizza, and many more. Within a ten mile radius of campus, there are more resurants than I can count. Some of my favorite are located in Sunset Plaza. The Big Cheese and Wall's Ice cream are a must.

◯ Great Location

Because UM is in Miami, the broad spectrum of dining experiences is available to students. The off-campus dining options can include high-end, fast-food, storts bars, and family atmospheres, and much more.

◯ Some Decent Restaurants.

In a walking distance, there are about 5 restaurants, and if you have a car, then there are lots of restaurants you can go.

◯ OK

You'll need a car for most places. Past midnight, drive thru or Denny's only.

◯ The Dinning Options Are Too Fancy for Me

In Miami there are different choices in food, but around UM there is not much for my tast. There is sushi which I don't eat often and chinese food. There is alot of high end dinning, but for a student with my fanacial shortage I cannot aford it. There is an organic store, but I by from Publix which I buy many of my foods close to my schools Publix.

◯ Cost

expensive food choices around school. only cheap stuff is mcdonalds.

The College Prowler Take On...
Off-Campus Dining

There aren't many cities that can match Miami as far as restaurants go. There is basically an endless amount of new places to try, and thankfully the quality of the restaurants matches up with the quantity of them. If you usually eat around Sunset Place, or on US-1, you can always head to Coconut Grove, South Beach, or downtown Coral Gables for a totally different selection of restaurants. All of these areas have numerous great restaurants, ranging from casual, cheap pizza and bar food, to expensive seafood or Italian. Students with cars like eating in the Grove, which also has shops, a movie theater, and lots of bars, providing for plenty of after-dinner entertainment. Even students without transportation will be impressed by the off-campus dining. There are dozens of restaurants right across the street at Sunset Place and in the surrounding area, not to mention what else becomes available if you're willing to risk a Metrorail ride.

Most students come to school without knowing a lot about Miami restaurants, and then they fall in love with a couple and frequent them for the next four years. The great thing about off-campus dining is that there is delivery available from so many places that almost every type of food can be covered. Besides pizza, there are also Mexican, Chinese, and Cuban restaurants that deliver. For quick 24-hour dining, it's about a five-minute to drive to Taco Bell or McDonald's. For larger meals at all hours, look for Denny's across the street, La Carreta and its various neighbors on Calle Ocho, or Jerry's Deli in South Beach, where there's never a shortage of things to do at any hour of the day.

A-

The College Prowler® Grade on

Off-Campus
Dining: A-

A high Off-Campus Dining grade implies that off-campus restaurants are affordable, accessible, and worth visiting. Other factors include the variety of cuisine and the availability of alternative options (vegetarian, vegan, kosher).

Campus Housing

The Lowdown On...
Campus Housing

On-Campus Housing Available?
Yes

Campus Housing Capacity
4,821

Average Housing Costs
$6,322

Number of Dormitories
5

Number of Campus-Owned Apartments
1

Dormitories

Eaton College

Floors: 4
Number of Occupants:
Approx. 400
Bathrooms: Shared between
rooms
Coed: Yes
Room Types: Suite single,
suite double
Special Features: Laundry,
study lounges on every floor

Hecht College

Floors: Two towers with 12
floors each
Number of Occupants:
Approx. 700
Bathrooms: Shared by floor
Coed: Yes
Room Types: Standard single,
standard double
Special Features: Laundry,
study lounge in lobby

Mahoney College

Floors: 7
Number of Occupants:
Approx. 700
Bathrooms: Shared between
rooms
Coed: Yes
Room Types: Suite single,
suite double
Special Features: Laundry,
study lounges, kitchens
shared by floor

Pearson College

Floors: 7
Number of Occupants:

Approx. 700
Bathrooms: Shared between
rooms
Coed: Yes
Room Types: Suite single,
suite double
Special Features: Laundry,
study lounges, kitchens
shared by floor

Stanford College

Floors: Two towers with 12
floors each
Number of Occupants:
Approx. 700
Bathrooms: Shared by floor
Coed: Yes
Room Types: Standardsingle,
standard souble
Special Features: Laundry,
study lounge in lobby

Campus-Owned Apartments

Apartment Area

Floors: 3
Number of Units: 12
Bathrooms: In-room
Coed: Yes
Residents: Upperclassmen
Room Types: Apartments
Special Features: Laundry
facilities between apartments

Freshmen Required to Live on Campus?

Yes

Undergrads Living On Campus

44%

Best Dorms

Eaton
Mahoney
Pearson

Worst Dorms

Hecht
Stanford

What You Get

Bed
Bookshelf
Cable TV
Closet
Desk and chair
Dresser
Ethernet access
Free campus and local phone
calls (phone not included)
Trash can
Window coverings

Available for Rent

Carts and vacuums are
available for loan.

Also Available

Apartment for single students
Fraternity/sorority housing

Quiet floors
Special housing for diabled
students
Theme housing

Did You Know?

The campus cable network was upgraded recently to include HBO and 60 other stations that are free to students.

There is at least one Resident Assistant living on each floor whose job it is to help new students feel comfortable and to encourage friendly relations among floormates.

Under a newly passed law in Florida, there is no smoking allowed in campus buildings, including the residential colleges. Picnic tables and benches are set up for smokers outside of each dorm.

Students Speak Out On...
Campus Housing

Q Hecht - the True Freshman Experience

If you are really looking for a freshman experience to the T, live in Hecht your first year. Yeah, Stanford is way more chill and the people are nicer, but Hecht has the comradorie that Stanford doesn't. People in Hecht are much hyper and there is always something fun to do. It cna get annoying after a while but as long as you have friends on your floor/tower, then you are set.

Q Dorm Life Is Best Freshman Year, Dorm Quality Gets Better With Age.

My first year I lived in Hecht, one of the Freshman towers, and it was insanely fun. It's a great opportunity to meet new friends and have the atypical first year experience in a safe environment, but the dorms are very small. I spent sophomore year in the Mahoney-Pearson dorms, which were certainly an upgrade, at least there were only 4 people to a bathroom as opposed to 60. Now, in my junior/senior year, I live in the University Village which is simply amazing. I could not imagine my college experience without dorm life, it's the best!

Q Close to Food

Living on campus lets you be close to the dining halls. Easy yum.

Q Friends Are Made

Living on campus provides a very interesting environment. I met most of my friends through on campus housing. Although the community bathroom was not ideal.

Q Housing Is Horrid

Campus housing is horrible when compared to what people normally think of when they think of life in Miami, and especially in the affluent Coral Gables. The freshmen dorms, Hecht & Stanford- also know as the towers, are tiny & cramped. Mahoney, Pearson & Eaton are only a little better with private bathrooms in the suites shared by 4 people & among the first choices for most students. Mahoney & Pearson are a bit more active than Eaton, which is a very quiet building in general, but not as active as the Towers where people are more focused on making friends and getting to know the neighbors. The best housing by far is University Village with it's gorgeous floor plans and featuring full kitchens. However they are reserved for upperclassmen and extremely hard to get into and much pricer than apartments in the surrounding off campus areas.

Q Not Very Good...

Rooms are very small and not very clean. But oh well..this is probably one of the few bad qualities about UM.

Q

I do not mind the dorms at all. In fact, I strongly recommend living on campus. It has been a lot of fun living with several people of different backgrounds, and I have enjoyed getting to know all of them. Some people complain about communal bathrooms, but they are cleaned twice a day. Other people complain about roommates, but I have not had a bad experience with my roommate.

Q

The dorms are typical, yet quite nice. It's impossible to avoid the community bathroom freshmen dorms, but once the first year is over, Eaton, Mahoney, and Pearson sport double suite-type rooms, each with their own bathroom.

The College Prowler Take On...
Campus Housing

If you decide to attend UM, there will be a form you fill out ranking the residential colleges by preference. This seems to be basically useless, as almost all freshmen are placed in Hecht or Stanford, also called the Towers. Although the other dorms are bigger and don't have communal bathrooms, most students agree that spending a year in the Towers is a good experience because it forces you to meet people. The suites in Mahoney, Pearson, and Eaton are nicer, but some students like the atmosphere in the Towers so much that they keep their rooms for the next year. The Towers are definitely the most wild and fun dorms, then Mahoney and Pearson, where some floors have a good social atmosphere. Eaton is generally considered the quietest of the residential colleges, which many people might prefer.

If you're lucky and you have a good RA, your floor will turn into a big family. Video game tournaments and hallway sports are common, and chances are, at least a few people on your floor will be friends that you keep in touch with for the rest of college. A lot of upperclassmen try to get into the apartments, which are tough to reserve. The layout is nice, but the buildings themselves are old and in random areas of campus where it's hard to meet new people. In the past, there have been overcrowding issues, and students have been sent to the Holiday Inn across the street from campus. Even though a free hotel room with maid service and HBO might sound like a good deal, avoid this at all costs if you have any desire to meet people and make friends.

B+

The College Prowler® Grade on

A high Campus Housing grade indicates that dorms are clean, well-maintained, and spacious. Other determining factors include variety of dorms, proximity to classes, and social atmosphere.

Off-Campus Housing

The Lowdown On...
Off-Campus Housing

Undergrads Living Off Campus
56%

Average Rents
Studio: $650
1 BR: $875
2 BR: $1,200
4 BR: $2,600

Best Time to Look for a Place
Beginning or middle of second semester

Popular Areas
Brickell/Downtown
Coral Gables
South Miami
University Village

Students Speak Out On...
Off-Campus Housing

Q Seems Like a Spa Resort

All off campus housing are fix up like if the area is a resort in a vacation spot. Even the apartments have bran new appliances and the rooms have recently been redone and freshly painted. Most places have a tennise court of a pool. Some even have a workout place in the housing area. There is more houses then apartments and looks very well kept. The housing here are nice, but like nice things it is expensive.

Q Good Apartments Are Hard to Get.

There are some very good options such as Red Road Commons and Valencia. It's not hard to find somewhere to live but some places are 12-month leases making them vastly more expensive than on-campus housing. Red Road is a great place to live from what I've seen but there's a long waiting list. Parking isn't too bad at the places. Bike distance for most people. Surrounding area is very safe for Red Road, not as much for Valencia. Brickell is very nice but expensive and far. Not worth the trouble. Houses can be a good way to go.

Q Coral Gables Housing

It's expensive, but if price is not an object it is really good because the CG area is very nice.

Q Great

I live with my parents ,cant get better than that. But I gave it B because of all the traffic there on on the way to UM. Its horrible.

Q It Costs a Lot.

Being in Miami, off-campus housing can be very costly unless you have many people living together.

Q A Decent Selection

With the recent housing crisis, many students have moved off campus, but now the closest apartments are all overflowing with students. Still, it's easy enough to find houses in the surrounding area, but some of the areas are kind of dangerous.

Q Is Luck on You Side?

There are a few well known places to look for off campus housing near the university. There is one large apartment complex with semi-reasonable prices that many students find shelter in, along with old houses that border the far reaches of the campus. Many students rent or buy these houses and live together splitting the cost. If you cannot afford the apartments and do not get lucky with a house going on the market you might find yourself stuck in the confines of a dorm.

Q On Your Own

Definitely consult with Miami natives before moving off campus. public transportation is iffy at best in MIami, and you do not want to end up living in a bad part of town.

The College Prowler Take On...
Off-Campus Housing

To be able to live on campus, students have to not only pay for their dorm rooms but also their meal plans. Such costs on top of tuition lead to a very hefty payment at the beginning of each semester. Since Miami has many available places to live off campus, it may turn out to be a better financial decision to not live in the dorms, especially if you are going to share rent with a group of friends. Nothing can beat having your own privacy and bring able to sleep without someone in the next room making a ruckus at 4 a.m. A private laundry facility and bathrooms that come with having your own space are also a plus.

However, when living off campus, students get separated from the social atmosphere that is present when living in a dorm, but this all depends on how social you are. Still, depending on how far away your apartment is, traffic on US 1 is an absolute nightmare. An accident can make a 10-minute drive drag out to 30 or even 45 minutes. The traffic is nothing compared to the bad drivers that are prevalent throughout Miami. Sometimes it looks as if some people have barely passed their driving test. There is definitely some serious road rage here.Living with friends and experiencing the freedom that comes with living off campus may be worth it to some, but traffic may close the deal on living in dorms for all four years for others.

B

The College Prowler® Grade on
Off-Campus
Housing: B

A high grade in Off-Campus Housing indicates that apartments are of high quality, close to campus, affordable, and easy to secure.

Diversity

The Lowdown On...
Diversity

African American
8%

Native American
0%

Asian American
5%

White
43%

Hispanic
23%

Unknown
12%

International
9%

Out-of-State Students
60%

Faculty Diversity

African American: 4%
Asian American: 10%
Hispanic: 21%
International: 12%
Native American: 0%
White: 53%
Unknown: 0%

Historically Black College/University?

No

Student Age Breakdown

Under 18: 1%
18-19: 27%
20-21: 31%
22-24: 20%
25+: 20%

Economic Status

Given the high cost of attending UM and the fancy clothing seen around campus, many students seem to come from wealthy homes. This doesn't mean that there aren't plenty of students with modest backgrounds, but those really struggling with finances may want to take into consideration the high cost of living in Miami.

Gay Pride

Miami is famous for its wide-spread homosexual culture, especially in the South Beach area. Citizens are very accepting of the gay community, and UM mirrors that tolerance with organizations like spectrUM.

Most Common Religions

The religions found at the University of Miami are as diverse as the students studying here. The most common religions found include Islam, Christianity, Judaism, and Hinduism.

Political Activity

The 2008 election invited a surge of political activity in the students at UM. Both President Barack Obama and Senator John McCain made a visit to Coral Gables, and much of the student population turned out to see them. While the political activity has wound down after the election, there are both Democratic and Republican student organizations on campus. For the most part, the political views are as diverse as the people here.

Minority Clubs on Campus

Minority students will feel right at home in the diverse atmosphere of Miami. Clubs like OASIS, Asian American Students Association, and African Students Union will help students meet others from their ethnic background.

Students Speak Out On...
Diversity

Q Students from Everywhere!
Talking about the diversity...no complain. There are students from seriously all over the world. You get to make world-wide friends.

Q Diversity Is Everywhere
You'd be hard pressed to find a more diverse campus anywhere in the US.

Q The Student Population Is Very Diverse.
The students are a mixture of many different ethnic groups as well as many age groups. Everyone is friendly and very helpful to each other. Everywhere you look you see a mixture of different ages and cultures talking, studying or just enjoying themselves. We help each other out whether it is with homework, studying for a test or loaning money for a snack. Even teachers can be found joining in.

Q Most Diverse Campus in the Country!
University of Miami boasts one of if not the most diverse campus in the country. We have students from every single state and more than 120 countries. When I walk to class, I often hear AT LEAST one other language besides Spanish and English. My friends are from all over the country and a few are from the other side of the world. I really get to know people who have grown up in completely different environments than me. I go to a school that pretty accurately represents the population of the nation as a whole, not just the region in which it is located.

Q Diversity

This college is extremely diverse. Miami is a melting pot of cultures. What a better place to show that than UM.

Q Diversity Yes and No

The U has a very eclectic racial diversity, many countries represented as well as a council just for international students called COISO. However the socio-economic diversity is very limited, most students have money and flaunt it with the help of their cars, clothes or electronics.

Q Diversity Is More Than Skin-Deep

Many freshman students I've encountered do not seem to notice that diversity at the University of Miami is a lot more subtle than just skin color and ethnic background. Everyone points to the racial/ethnic diversity on campus, but I find that the diversity in religion, in character, and in past experiences are more valuable. If you are trying to fit in with a particular crowd, you are going to have a hard time being accepted, but if you are whatever you feel like being, you will find a variety of people along the way who you can click with. As a first-year, I recommend getting involved with the First Year U Program, the IMPACT Retreat, and STRIVE, a volunteer organization. You get to meet and interact with people on a level way past just the introductory "Where are you from" and "What's your major" questions.There are many people from a high-income background, but half of the class of 2014 is on a merit-based scholarship. Most of the people you meet will care about their grades, even if they lack the discipline to obtain those grades. You can see people running up high costs to support their social life, but there are many free events on campus, and the front desks in the residence halls are always offering free tickets to something every weekend.

Q I read somewhere that we have one of the most diverse campuses in the United States, and that's evident from just walking around campus for a short amount of time.

The College Prowler Take On...
Diversity

Like most big cities, Miami has areas that are very cultural, and visiting these areas might feel like stepping into another world. Instead of Chinatown, Miami has Little Havana, the world's largest collection of Cubans outside of Cuba. The huge Hispanic population in Miami is not limited to one area. You'll overhear conversations spoken in Spanish almost everywhere in the city, and sometimes the accents are hard to understand and you end up with totally preposterous things in your McDonald's bag after an unsuccessful trip to the drive-thru. Most students get accustomed to Miami's Hispanic heritage pretty quickly and take advantage of the great atmosphere of Calle Ocho, the street that runs through the heart of Little Havana.

Miami has so many different ethnicities represented that students coming from non-diverse backgrounds may feel uncomfortable at first. As the numbers prove, only half of the students in most classes will be white. This is a great experience for students of any ethnicity. It basically forces you to understand different cultures and people from various backgrounds. It's especially interesting to hear what students from other countries write in English class when culture plays a major part. There are also various religions represented. Christian clubs are popular, as are other religious organizations like Hillel. Homosexual students will also feel right at home, especially in South Beach, a hotspot for gay culture. Don't come to Miami expecting to be surrounded by the same people you would at a school in Iowa. UM is one of the most diverse campuses in the nation, and some students find this to be the best thing about life in Miami.

The College Prowler® Grade on

Diversity: A

A high grade in Diversity indicates that ethnic minorities and international students have a notable presence on campus and that students of different economic backgrounds, religious beliefs, and sexual preferences are well-represented.

Guys & Girls

The Lowdown On...
Guys & Girls

Female Undergrads
53%

Male Undergrads
47%

Birth Control Available?

Yes: Condoms are always available for free in a basket at the Student Health Center, and there are conferences and campaigns to promote awareness of teen pregnancy and birth control methods.

Social Scene

The school is very social, and most guys and girls don't have trouble meeting people if they want to. Since almost all freshmen live in the Towers their first year, they will often meet other students on their floor when they share bathroom facilities. Usually guys and girls live on alternate floors, so the opposite sex is never too far away. Since most students come to UM looking to make friends, it's never hard to find someone to hang out with, even if it takes a couple weeks to build stronger friendships.

Hookups or Relationships?

As is expected, most freshmen come to school without being in relationships. Random hookups are common in the beginning, but after a few months or a year, relationships take over. Miami is a great town for dating, with plenty of romantic spots and restaurants.

Dress Code

The clothing seen on campus is almost as diverse as the students that go here. For every guy that falls out of bed five minutes before class and throws on sandals and jeans, there's a girl wearing the latest fashions to her math lectures. For daily life, pretty much anything goes. Most of the guys stick with shorts and T-shirts during the day, and the girls wear jeans and tank tops. Bring some preppy clothes for going out at night, when the standard dress is slacks and formal shirts for guys, and skirts and nice tops for girls. The heaviest thing you'll need as far as the weather goes is a hooded sweatshirt and jeans. Make sure to bring a comfortable pair of sandals—a UM staple for both guys and girls.

Did You Know?

Top Places to Find Hotties:
1. Any beach in Miami
2. Campus swimming pool
3. The Rat

Top Places to Hook Up:
1. South Beach
2. Bars or clubs in Coconut Grove
3. House parties
4. Fraternities/sororities
5. Coed dorms

Q Campus Life
The students at UA are from all over the country. Easy to mingle. Great football team and special events.

Q EXTREMELY Attractive Student Body
The students at UM are, what can I say - very attractive. As a result, there are a lot of "dude bros" and skanky girls. However, there is no shortage of beautiful, down to earth guys and girls here. You just have to make friends according to your taste. Since there is so much diversity, there are tons of different kinds of people with different interest that are bound to match your own.

Q Girls Are Hot
It's the University of Miami. The majority of the students are girls, and the majority of them are gorgeous.For both guys and girls, you'll get some genuine people but a lot of douches as well.

Q Good Looking Campus.
We're a diverse bunch at the University of Miami-- it's not all the superficial South Beach crowd. There are plenty of bronzed bodies with big brains to go around!

Q Different for Everyone
Yes, the girls are hot.Yes, the guys are fairly attractive. The hotness of girls at the U is hyped because of the setting and because of the number of 10's on campus. The average girl is barely more attractive than the average girl at another school. We just happen to have some gorgeous girls who flaunt what they were blessed with in bikini's in the center of campus at the pool. They're

generally interested in going clubbing and seeing famous people in Miami. Dress sometimes screams "I'm very rich and everyone should know it." Social life is much like any college setting: Girls have all the power and guys will throw drinks and money their way in hopes of ending up with them at the end of the night.Relationships are a rarity past a one night association. If you can find someone you are attracted to AND you can bare to talk to for more than fifteen minutes, ask them out immediately. It's a 1 in a 1000 chance you find someone like that.The guys are a large mix. Athletic to un-athletic. Attractive to hideous. Snobby to the most down-to-earth guy you ever met. Pretty much every type of guy exists here.

Q Turn Lesbian

The guys are nothing special at all...The girls are ok-looking but with the skimpy clothing they wear all the time, UM is a guy's fantasy

Q All girls here are the pretty, superficial, bubbly, annoyingly preppy type who partied all through high school, while still managing to be in NHS and graduate with honors. You will wonder how people got into this school. Boys are a male version of this. There is a lot of sex.

Q The guys are pretty good, a lot of real Jersey boys and Long Islanders. The girls are very attractive and from all over the country.

The College Prowler Take On...
Guys & Girls

The opinion of most UM students seems to be that the student body's bodies are great to look at, but that this is not a school to meet your future spouse. Temporary flings or random hooking up is common among freshmen who are basking in their post-high school freedom. But once everyone gets settled and makes the friends they'll have for the next four years, relationships kick in. There are plenty of great places around Miami to take a date, as far as restaurants and nightspots go. But finding someone on campus who fulfills your emotional needs, as well as your physical ones, might prove challenging. Perhaps the biggest problem is that guys and girls hide their real identities in favor of tight clothes and good tans, since that seems to be the look most students are going for.

The school can be as promiscuous as you want it to be. If you're looking for a quick hook up, it's not hard to head to a bar or club. Most students don't make this a habit, as it obviously complicates things a great deal. Your best bet is to make a bunch of friends that are the opposite sex in the beginning of your freshman year, and then you'll have plenty of connections to guys or girls for the rest of college. Overall, the guys and girls look great, and to be fair, some are great all around. But the amount of really intelligent, nice, caring people who are also hot seems to be low. Many other colleges face the opposite situation, so you have to ask yourself if you're looking for long-term relationships in college, or if you just want to have some fun with no commitment.

The College Prowler®
Grade on
Guys & Girls

A high grade for Guys or Girls indicates that the students on campus is attractive, smart, friendly, and engaging, and that the school has a decent gender ratio.

Guys: A

Girls: B+

Athletics

The Lowdown On...
Athletics

Athletic Association
NAA
NCAA

Athletic Division
NCAA Division I-A

Athletic Conferences
Football: Atlantic Coast
Conference
Basketball: Atlantic Coast
Conference

School Colors
Orange and green

**School Nickname/
Mascot**
Sebastion the Ibis

**Men Playing Varsity
Sports**
227: 5%

Women Playing Varsity Sports

282: 6%

Men's Varsity Sports

Baseball
Basketball
Diving
Football
Tennis
Track and field

Women's Varsity Sports

Basketball
Golf
Rowing
Soccer
Swimming and diving
Tennis
Track and field
Volleyball

Intramurals

Basketball
Dodgeball
Flag football
Floor hockey
Golf
Racquetball
Soccer
Softball
Table tennis
Tennis
Ultimate Frisbee
Volleyball
Wallyball
Wiffleball

Club Sports

Aikido
Badminton
Baseball
Body building/weightlifting
Bowling
Brazilina Jiu-Jitsu
Canes Outdoor Recreation Program
Dance
Dodgeball
Equestrian
Fencing
Field hockey
Golf
Karate
Lacrosse
Racquetball
Rock climbing
Roller hockey
Rugby
Sailing
Scuba
Soccer
Softball (fastpitch)
Squash
Swimming
Table tennis
Tae Kwon Do
Tennis
Triathlon
Ultimate Frisbee
Volleyball
Wakeboarding
Water polo
Whiffleball

Students Receiving Athletic Financial Aid

Football: 81

Basketball: 24
Baseball: 20
Cross Country/Track: 38
Other Sports: 92

Graduation Rates of Athletic Financial Aid Recipients
Football: 53%
Basketball: 29%
Baseball: 50%
Cross Country/Track: 100%
Other Sports: 70%

Athletic Fields & Facilities
Alex Rodriguez Park
Bank United Center
Cobb Stadium
GreenTree Practice Fields
Hecht Athletic Center
Hurricane Strength & Conditioning Center
IM Fields
James L. Knight Sports Complex
Neil Schiff Tennis Center
Norman Witten Student Union Pool
Ronald W. Shane Watersports Center
Sun Life Stadium
Wellness Center

Most Popular Sports

Football dominates every weekend during the season, with students spending Saturday afternoons supporting the team. The baseball team is also one of the country's best, but it doesn't get nearly the amount of attention that football does.

Most Overlooked Teams

The women's basketball team is among the top in its division, and even in the country, but few pay attention to it. The baseball team gets great recognition nationally, but you're more likely to see Sportscenter anchors talking about it than you are to hear it in a conversation among students.

School Spirit

A popular chant at football games says, "It's great to be a Miami Hurricane!" Most students seem to feel this way, with plenty of school-related things to be proud of. The sports teams, notably football and baseball, are always among the top in the nation. The weather is great, the people are gorgeous, and the campus is beautiful. Shirts or hats with the school logo or colors on them are fairly common, as are cool little items like UM slippers, car magnets, and school supplies. Since UM is the only major college in the area, there is no direct rival other than schools from central or northern Florida like UF or FSU. Sporting events against these opponents attract huge crowds, while games against lesser-known opponents like Rutgers might have students sleeping in or heading to the beach instead.

Getting Tickets

Attending UM is a sports-lover's dream. Students get free access to any UM sporting event with their ID card. Tickets to football bowl games are also available for students to purchase, and the school puts together packages to allow students to attend away games during football season. The basketball arena and baseball stadium on campus are fun places to see a game for free.

Best Place to Take a Walk

The path around the lake, or the road that circles the school are very scenic places to take walks.

Students Speak Out On...
Athletics

Q Cane Football
Football at the you is just like takeing a breath,without you would survive. everyonr supports the team on good and bad days,just dont see hoe i could go wrong by not participating.

Q The U Invented Swagger
The teams aren't always the best, but we have swagger

Q Best Football Team
The university of Miami has great spirit toward the powerful football team Hurricane

Q We All Say GO CANES
There aren't many people that don't go to the games. Even people who have no idea about college football appreciate the Miami Hurricanes

Q Athletics Are the Ish
Despite not winning our Bowl game this year, you ahve to realize that UM is getting back on top as far as sports. Our Womens Basketball team is in the NIT Finals! Come on now! Athletics here are one of my favorite events to go to. There are always live and you can meet new friends who share the same interests in sports.

Q Umiami Sports Are...
At university of Miami, the sports are taken very seriously by the students and even faculty. Our sports teams are followed by almost everyone associated with the university, which gives a feeling of camaraderie throughout the entire

town. Our facilities are open to every student and are top of the line as well. We fall short in that our basketball team does not get enough recognition and that we don't have a male varsity soccer team, but our club sports make up for that. It seems like a high percentage of our student body participates in some sort of club or intramural sport.

ℚ Not the Same U

I love our football team. A lot of people love our football team. I like our baseball team and basketball team too. Student involvement is fairly easy. You can get into games for free and the Exercise and Sport Sciences in the School of Education has many oportunities to work with our teams.Team performance: Football is exciting and very skilled, Basketball is a talented group who can't always keep up in the ACC and tend to blow games in the second half. Baseball is top notch most years.Fan support: What happened to the Orange Bowl? Fan support disappeared after it was knocked down. Alumni must move away because we can't seem to sell out a game. Oklahoma game this year was near full but with some seats covered. Smaller games like Florida A&M are lucky to get the stadium 1/3 full. Basketball support is non-existent. Baseball gets a pretty big crowd at most games.School spirit: Swag seems to be something that no one has yet everyone boasts. My experience of the school spirit is that most people wear a jersey, throw up the []_[] and call themselves a die-hard fan. The girls won't and don't care and most guys care. The only thing is that only a select few care enough to make it to every game and yell the whole time.Athletic facilities: I hear they're nice... wouldn't know. The wellness center is pretty nice. It's getting expanded right now too.LandShark Stadium/Dolphin Stadium/Sunlife Stadium sucks. 45 minute bus ride away, pro-style seems rather different when college teams are playing, and it's just too big for us to fill.

Q Can Be Good, but Falling Off

Traditionally we have an amazing football, basketball and baseball team, but each has faltered recently. But going to the football games is usually a lot of fun, and shuttles are provided. Basketball and Baseball take place on campus.

The College Prowler Take On...
Athletics

Although UM students might be lazy when it comes to academics, politics, or national events, one thing they take seriously is football. One thing that UM students treat religiously is football. God help you if you come in between a 'Cane and the TV if the game is on. It helps, of course, that UM has one of the most dominant college football programs in the country and that the team shows no sign of dropping out of the nation's top tier. A true sign of a college student's devotion is how early they're willing to wake up for a game. For 12 p.m. games on Saturdays, students line up outside the gates of Dolphin Stadium as early as 8 a.m. to ensure good seats. By the mid-morning, the lines wind out into the parking lot. This is especially true for the big games against rivals like the University of Florida or Florida State University. Tickets to every UM sport are free to students, but not many people bother with anything but football, even though one of our former athletes took part in the 2008 Beijing Olympics.

Intramurals also play a big part in campus life. There's a yearly competition between the residential colleges called Sportsfest, where teams from the dorms compete in dozens of games over a weekend. There are also intramurals during the fall and the spring, where the activity is dominated by fraternities, but can also include various other organizations. The IM games get pretty heated, especially in popular sports like flag football and basketball. Sportsfest is a fun way to compete against other dorms and other floors from within your building, and it also helps to build bonds between floormates. But the most important thing will always be the football team, proven by the funeral-like silence the day after any rare loss.

B+

The College Prowler® Grade on

Athletics: B+

A high grade in Athletics indicates that students have school spirit, that sports programs are respected, that games are well-attended, and that intramurals are a prominent part of student life.

Nightlife

The Lowdown On...
Nightlife

Cheapest Place to Get a Drink
The Tavern

Primary Areas with Nightlife
Coconut Grove
South Beach

Closing Time
3 a.m.

Useful Resources for Nightlife
Miami New Times
Street Magazine
www.cityvibz.com/
miamimiamiclubs.shtml

Club Listings

B.E.D.
929 Washington Ave.
South Beach
(305) 532-9070
www.bedmiami.com
B.E.D. is a rare example of when a theme-reliant club succeeds. This club has grown to be one of the top spots in South Beach, due largely to the innovative idea of serving patrons dinner not at tables or chairs, but in bed. If you don't come with enough people, you might have to share your bed with another party, which isn't always a bad thing. Ordering from the fancy menu is mandatory upon entry, and food alone can cost you $50, not including the drink minimums. Sunday: Closed. Sample theme nights include: Secret Society R&B and Hip Hop, Disco Jazz Night, Abstrakt Fridays—Vintage Funk & Soul, SKIN—Rock-Dance Mix

Crobar
1445 Washington Ave.
South Beach
(305) 531-8225
www.crobarmiami.com
Crobar is one of the more popular clubs in South Beach, but it's not really considered one of the best. Its location on a crowded corner in the heart of SoBe certainly adds to its popularity, but the majority of students seem to try Crobar once and settle into some lesser-known, yet nicer, South Beach nightspot. Hours: 10 p.m-5 a.m. Capactity: 1200. Ages: 21+

Nikki Beach
1 Ocean Dr.
South Beach
(305) 538-1111
www.nikkibeach.com
This outdoor beach club is a refreshing alternative to the crowded, sweaty dark rooms featured in other clubs. Nikki Beach is a cross between club and resort. The partying literally never stops, as you can always find people out in the mornings and afternoons enjoying cocktails and the sights of the beautiful people around them. This spot is considered one of the most exclusive clubs in Miami, so entry will probably be denied to most college students; those who get in never want to leave. This club has more of a tourist and visitor crowd, because anyone who lived this 24-hour hedonistic lifestyle for more than a couple days would probably get burnt out pretty quickly. Sample features include: Sushi hour, Retro '80s,

"Winter in Miami," Indio Loco, New-Style Brunch, "Tangerine Dreams"

Opium

136 Collins Ave.
South Beach
(305) 531-5535
www.opiummiami.com
Yet another South Beach hotspot, Opium competes mainly with clubs like Crobar, Space, Level, and the tons of other popular places. Opium advertises a lot with fliers around campus, and so it appears to be more popular at first glance. Opium is one of the big-name clubs, like Crobar, that everyone has to try once, but most people end up going to a smaller spot.

Bar Listings

Monty's

2550 S. Bayshore Dr.
Coconut Grove
(305) 858-1431
www.montysstonecrab.com
Monty's is a tough sell for those who've never been there. The location, although in the Grove, is pretty far removed from the heart of the bar scene. The most popular area is out on the deck by the water, which clashes with the dark, smoky atmosphere of most of the local drinking spots. But Monty's is one of the hottest locales for early evening drinking, especially with mixed drinks like the Painkiller. This isn't really a late-night hangout, so there aren't many specials or theme nights, but few weekends go by without gathering on the deck at Monty's for "pre-gaming."

Mr. Moe's

3131 Commodore Plaza
Coconut Grove
(305) 442-1114
www.mrmoes.com
Mr. Moe's has a pretty cool log cabin décor and the attitude to match. Wednesday nights are especially interesting with a bull riding theme, and Karaoke night on Tuesdays is always fun. Like a lot of other bars, Mr. Moe's has happy hour every night from 11 a.m.-8 p.m., and features a ton of TVs for sporting events. The food is actually pretty good, and fairly cheap for the Grove, and so the place stays open as a restaurant during the day before turning into the typical bar at night, with a mid-western slant.

Sandbar

3064 Grand Ave.
Coconut Grove
(305) 444-5270
www.sandbargrill.com
Sandbar, is a top destination for UM students looking to drink and have a good time without the hectic pace of a club in South Beach. For the most part a bar is a bar, but Sandbar stays popular because of its specials and theme nights. The White Trash Bash every Tuesday is a fun theme for students with hokey trailer park attire on hand, and $1.50 cans. The biggest weeknight for a college bar is Thursday, so Sandbar offers $3 bottles and a special late-night happy hour from 2 a.m.-5 a.m. with $2 bottles. Other specials include Monday night football and Karaoke Wednesdays.

The Tavern

3416 Main Hwy.
Coconut Grove
(305) 447-3884
www.tavernmiami.com
This favorite of UM students is known for its cheap drinks, generous specials, and fairly lenient ID checking. There's a happy hour every weeknight before 8 p.m., but the best special is all-you-can-drink on Monday nights for $10.

Other nights basically feature various beers at cheap prices, except for Sunday night, when the combination of $5 pitchers and beer pong ensures an interesting evening.

Titanic

5813 Ponce De Leon Blvd.
Coral Gables
(305) 667-2537
www.titanicbrewery.com
Titanic is rare for a Miami bar in that it's not in the Grove or South Beach. But this spot became popular because of its location right next to campus, and because it's the only bar within reasonable walking distance of UM. It has become popular with the UM crowd because of its great live music, relaxed atmosphere, and lack of a cover charge. Titanic brews its own beer, some of which it names after UM traditions, and there are plenty of specials and happy hour drinks. With no cover charge, and no minimum age for entry, it won't hurt to walk down the street and give Titanic a try.

Other Places to Check Out
Club Space
Deep
Delano
Fat Tuesday's
Level
Life
Quench
Señor Frog's
Space
Tobacco Road
Ultra Lounge
Voyage
Wet Willie's

Favorite Drinking Games
Beer pong
Card games
Century Club
Power Hour
Quarters

What to Do if You're Not 21
Books and Books
265 Aragon Ave.
Coral Gables
(305) 442-4408
www.booksandbooks.com
Okay, so hanging out at a bookstore probably doesn't appeal
to the bar and club crowd, but if you're into art or writing or
poetry, then you'll want to make Books and Books a priority.
This 20-year-old independent bookstore was a hit with locals
long before Barnes and Noble became a nationally-recog-
nized name. The location in beautiful downtown Coral Gables
has hosted an incredible list of celebrity authors and poets
like Martin Ames, Allen Ginsburg, Jamaica Kincaid, Salman
Rushdie, Kurt Vonnegut, Judy Blume, Walter Cronkite, Dave
Barry, Carl Hiaasen, Jimmy Carter, Al Gore, Rudy Giuliani,
Rosie O'Donnell, Cindy Crawford, and Mariel Hemingway. The

store keeps a pretty up-to-date listing of upcoming readings and events on its Web site, so be sure to check and see if anyone cool is coming soon. Books and Books also looks to entertain its loyal patrons with live music and a nice café.

Café Demetrio
300 Alhambra Circle
Coral Gables
(305) 448-4949
www.cafedemetrio.com
Although you won't find wild dancing and barely-dressed hotties at this coffeehouse, Café Demetrio provides a quiet but cool atmosphere for students who prefer coffee and a good book to blaring techno tunes and fake IDs. This quaint coffee bar in downtown Coral Gables is popular among the artsy crowd and brings in live bands to spice things up on Friday and Saturday nights. There's even a chess tournament night on the first Monday of every month. Make sure to check out the gourmet coffee and snacks at this local landmark.

Organization Parties
The only organizations throwing popular parties around campus are the fraternities, who host events at their houses on occasion. If there are other parties, you'll find a flyer on your windshield, under the door of your room, or jammed into the side of your car. The only other groups who would even think about trying to compete with the clubs and bars in the area are the school newspaper and radio station, who sometimes partner to sponsor house parties.

Students Speak Out On...
Nightlife

Q Party It up

Since this is Miami there are tons of clubs available for both the 21+ crowd and the 18+ crowd. If you don't mind the cab fare, South Beach is the place to be. Otherwise there are a good selection of clubs and bars in Coconut Grove which is much closer to the school. There are also a pretty good amount of house/frat parties always going on-- if you don't mind cheap beer and potentially crappy music. It's nice because the focus of nightlife here is not these parties, but rather the Miami club scene. Sometimes we do "takeovers" where you can get discounts and pretty much the whole school comes and, well, takes over the club. These nights are always fun.

Q Best Nightlife for Any School

Nightlife at University of Miami revolves around the Grove, South Beach, and Downtown Miami. There are so many venues, bars, and clubs you can experience. While the scene requires you to be 21 or get a hold of a fake ID, it is extremely fun and exciting. Getting to and from is a bit annoying. There is a shuttle from campus to the Grove on Thursday and Friday nights, but anywhere else you need a cab or car.

Q Welcome to Miami

From Coconut Grove to Miami Beach, the University of Miami offers its students a culturally diverse atmosphere with plenty of different scenes and events. There are festivals, concerts, Heat and Marlins games, clubs, bars, movies, bonfires, house parties, and so much more. The University of Miami even provides transportation to most of the events available! It's great to be a Miami Hurricane.

◯ The Grove, Sobe, Etc...

The grove can be pretty creepy as far as walking around with a bunch of friends. Unless you have a fake, you will either need to spit out the cash or show some body to get into a bar/club except on Thursday, especially in SoBe. I stick to parites thrown by MCG on campus because they are 18+, close to campus, and always fun or i go downtown and party there. It all just depends on what you are looking for. Miami is what you make it!

◯ Pretty Good

House parties of the better frats are exclusive to brothers. Lower tier frats let people in but it's 5-10 dollars for guys and free for girls.Clubs: From crappy to extravagant. Generally the nicer it is, the most strict on IDs they are. South Beach central.Bars: They're pretty much everywhere. You'll always be able to find a place where you can get in, it just might not be the place you really wanted to go. Coconut Grove central.

◯ Plenty of Nightlife

Plenty of frat parties and house parties, almost any night of week within walking distance from campus. South Beach is always a great option for clubs/dancing,need to rely on a cab or a friend with a car. the Grove is fun for bars, drinking, pretty easy to get in if underage, some 18+ places, caters specifically to the college crowd, school shuttle goes there on Thursday nights.

◯ Umiami Night Life

There is a lot to do off campus during the evening. The only thing about that is that you have to do some research and testing out of areas because it's not laid out in front of you. Most clubs are 21 and older so it would be wise for the 18 to 20 years old to make their own entertainment during the nights and weekends or see what the school is hosting. Cabs are easily accessible but are very costly.

Q Ehh

You must have a really good fake to go anywhere really. The house parties are always off campus so you have to take a cab to get anywhere in miami which is annoying and pricey. If you are into the club scene this is the school for you but if not it does not offer much. There is always something going on but usually the house parties get busted by 2 and they are too crowded to really do anything if you get it. Boys will find it really difficult to get into frats

The College Prowler Take On...
Nightlife

If you have any interest in coming to Miami for college, you've probably already heard about the nightlife. Celebrities flock to South Beach every weekend to party at some of the hottest clubs in the world, with UM students dancing by their sides. The Miami area has two primary areas for nightlife. First, there's Coconut Grove, which is mostly composed of shops, restaurants, and bars, and is about a 10-minute drive from campus. Most of the popular bars students attend are located here. Truly serious partiers will head to the clubs and 24-hour party atmosphere of South Beach, one of Miami's most famous cultural areas and a fixture in the nightlife scene of South Florida.

There are other, quieter bars around campus, but to say you're "going out" at UM generally means either SoBe or the Grove. Attire for South Beach is usually pretty chic, depending on the theme of the club you're hitting up. For the bars in the Grove, dress however you feel. There are some great drink specials in the Grove, and it doesn't take long to hear from friends which spots are carding and which don't mind a decent fake ID. South Beach is absurdly expensive, which reflects the ritzy crowd it attracts nightly. You'll want at least a few $20s whenever you head to South Beach, and that may only get you in the door and a couple of overpriced drinks. If you figure out when the specials and happy hours are in the Grove, you can make a few bucks go a long way. The bars in the Grove are most popular on weekends and Thursday nights, but South Beach never slows down. As far as other parties go, most are outshined by the excellent spots around town, but there are usually a few house parties just outside campus that survive.

The College Prowler® Grade on
Nightlife: A

A high grade in Nightlife indicates that there are many bars and clubs in the area that are easily accessible and affordable. Other determining factors include the number of options for the under-21 crowd and the prevalence of house parties.

Greek Life

The Lowdown On...
Greek Life

Undergrad Men in Fraternities
14%

Number of Sororities
13

Undergrad Women in Sororities
14%

Number of Fraternities
17

Fraternities

Alpha Phi Alpha
Alpha Sigma Phi
Beta Theta Pi
Kappa Alpha Psi
Lambda Chi Alpha
Lambda Theta Phi
Omega Psi Phi
Phi Beta Sigma
Phi Delta Theta
Pi Kappa Alpha
Pi Kappa Phi
Sigma Alpha Epsilon
Sigma Alpha Mu
Sigma Chi
Sigma Lambda Beta
Sigma Phi Epsilon
Zeta Beta Tau

Sororities

Alpha Delta Pi
Alpha Kappa Alpha
Delta Delta Delta
Delta Gamma
Delta Phi Epsilon
Delta Sigma Theta
Kappa Kappa Gamma
Lambda Theta Alpha
Sigma Delta Tau
Sigma Gamma Rho
Sigma Lambda Gamma
Zeta Phi Beta
Zeta Tau Alpha

Multicultural Colonies

Alpha Kappa Alpha (NPHC)
Alpha Phi Alpha (NPHC)
Delta Epsilon Psi (South
Asian Fraternity)

Delta Sigma Theta (NPHC)
Kappa Alpha Psi (NPHC)
Lambda Theta Alpha (LGC)
Lambda Theta Phi (LGC)
Omega Psi Phi (NPHC)
Phi Beta Sigma (NPHC)
Phi Iota Alpha (NALFO)
Sigma Gamma Rho (NPHC)
Sigma Lambda Beta (NALFO)
Sigma Lambda Gamma (LGC)
Zeta Phi Beta (NPHC)

Other Greek Organizations

Alpha Lambda Delta
Association of Greek Letter
Organizations
Gamma Sigma Alpha
Interfraternity Council
Latino Greek Council
National Panhellenic Council
Omicron Delta Kappa
Order of Omega
Rho Lambda

Did You Know?

The 26 percent of students who are Greek hold 85 percent of the campus leadership positions.

UM has a strict anti-hazing policy and monitors all Greek organizations during rush and pledge period.

Most UM fraternities and sororities participate in two major competitions per year. In the fall, there's Homecoming, when the organizations battle for victory by attending volunteer events, building floats, and staging skits called Organized Cheer. The big event of the spring is Greek Week, when similar events are held, along with more sports-oriented games and contests.

Students Speak Out On...
Greek Life

Q You get out what you put in

It's UM--why would you not expect diversity from its Greek life too?? Some might be quick to tell you that the Greek life at UM doesn't matter but anyone who's in a fraternity/sorority/multicultural will tell you that what you get out of it depends on what you put in. There are the stereotypes present in each group, but don't quickly write off all Greeks as that because there's so much more that goes on within the Greek system. There's more to it than just a social life. It's worth trying if you're even the slightest bit interested.

Q Greek Life at UM

It doesn't matter if you are in Sorority/Fraternity, because there are tons of party to go anyways. There is no difference if you are in a Greek life or not. You get along with people who are in Greek life also.

Q Present

There is greek life and they have some presence in the social scene, but it is in no way considered the "popular" thing to do. In some cases you can be more socially active if you're not in a frat or sorority because you won't be tied down by greek events.

Q Greeks Are Not Well Respected

There is a shortage of African American students on the University of Miami campus, which in turn causes Greek life to look less than alive. There are many different Greek organizations but there is no real diversity in the organizations which make the organizations look plain

& generic. There's nothing that really pops out because everyone seems the same. They put on great shows though.

Q Meh

Greek life is not huge at the U. Because of the rich Miami nightlife, frat parties are not a huge component of the social scene. Greek life seems to be more of a status thing and a lot of the people do fit the negative stereotypes people usually have about Greek life, but then again some people are the total opposite. It really is no big deal if you go Greek here or not because there are so many other things to do.

Q Minimal

The few frats there are have houses but there are no sorority houses. The most i see of sororities is them wearing shirts around campus. What is nice about them is that rush is in 2nd semester so you can wait and see how things work out before you commit to a sorority.

Q Greeks Don't Run Miami

The Greeks are definitely present, but they aren't as big as they are at other schools. The Greek parties aren't as big due to the variety of things there are to do in Miami.

Q

The Greek scene tries to make themselves seem all elusive and all, but no one really cares. The NPHC is very secretive, and they exist on campus, but it's hard to find them. They start coming out around spring time because we have deferred recruitment.

The College Prowler Take On...
Greek Life

Greek life is not a disruptive force on campus, but it is sizeable enough to make a difference. Although UM does not have the massive Greek system in place at some universities, there are plenty of fraternities and sororities for students to choose from. If you want to stay away from Greek life, you won't have to try hard at UM. The fraternity houses are lined on a road on the edge of campus, and the sorority and fraternity suites are in a building in a quiet part of UM. If not for the letter shirts seen around school, non-Greek students could easily forget that there are even fraternities and sororities at UM. But behind the scenes, the Greek system here is very important.

The social aspect of Greek life is present at UM, but is not overwhelming. The fraternities host parties occasionally at their houses, but UM's real social scene can be found at the bars and clubs in Miami. For the most part, Greeks hang out with other Greeks. The fraternities and sororities compete against each other in intramurals and Homecoming events, as well as a yearly competition called Greek Week. There is certainly a bond that exists between members of the Greek community, as well as a strong sense of pride and competition with other Greek organizations. If you've been studying episodes of MTV's Fraternity Life in preparation for college, you may want to look elsewhere. But if you want a Greek system that is quiet but still important, you will like UM's.

The College Prowler® Grade on

Greek Life: C+

A high grade in Greek Life indicates that sororities and fraternities are not only present, but also active on campus. Other determining factors include the variety of houses available and the respect the Greek community receives from the rest of the campus.

Drug Scene

The Lowdown On...
Drug Scene

Most Popular Drugs
Alcohol
Cocaine
Ecstasy
Marijuana

Alcohol-Related Referrals
371

Alcohol-Related Arrests
1

Drug-Related Referrals
64

Drug-Related Arrests
7

Drug Counseling Programs

BACCHUS (Boosting Alcohol Consciousness Concerning the Health of University Students)
Alcohol education in regards to college students

PIER21
(305) 284-6120
Alcohol and drug education, prevention, and intervention

Student Counseling Center
(305) 284-5511
General psychological counseling service, referrals to specialized counseling

Students Speak Out On...
Drug Scene

Q Whatever You Want
Most people drink and smoke weed. If you want to stay away from it, it is very possible. If you are looking for something more, you can find it too. I go to plenty of parties and do not drink and I feel comfortable. Most people say it, but it is true, it is really what you want to make of it.

Q Two Words: South Beach
There is plenty of drug use to go around, especially cocaine at the clubs. You cannot go too far without hearing at least one person talking about using adderol to study/pull an all-nighter. There is not that much peer pressure, but if you have an easily influenced personality, the pervasiveness and ease of acquisition will make you an easy target. Drinking is very popular, Friday morning classes are invariably full of hungover students from all demographics.

Q Peer Pressure
not too much peer pressure. however depends on personality

Q Drugs?
I don't really know if people do drugs here. I see some people doing marijuanas in their rooms sometimes, but nothing serious.

Q The Usual

I don't know all that much about the drug scene at UM because I don't participate. It mostly consists of drinking although there do seem to be a lot of people who smoke weed.

Q Drinking

There is a slight drug scene on campus, mainly pills to keep you awake and more focused as well as cigarettes. Drinking is a much more popular activity but it is punished severely when caught drinking underage.

Q Blatantely Obvious

People seriously walk around smelling like drugs everyday. They have "spots" that they go smoke in that are out in the open yet they don't get caught. Even in the dorms where drugs are prohibited, people still smoke, drink and much more in their room.

Q

There is a drug problem on campus. Many of the students are wealthy and think they have nothing better to spend daddy's money on than marijuana or crack, or alcohol for that matter.

The College Prowler Take On...
Drug Scene

College mirrors reality in that if you want drugs, you can always find them. Miami, like any big city, has its fair share of bad neighborhoods and drug addicts. But it's easy to stay away from them, especially around the campus in upscale Coral Gables. The only drug being really abused on UM's campus is alcohol, and that's true of almost all colleges. There are groups of students that are into marijuana, cocaine, ecstasy, or various other drugs, but dealing is not really a problem on campus, and most RAs are pretty strict about looking out for drug use in the dorms. Given UM's fairly difficult classes, most hardcore drug users aren't going to be around for long.

Most students don't seem worried about drugs on campus. While UM isn't going to make any top-10 lists of schools with drug problems, there is certainly a dependency on alcohol at social events and in the lives of most students. Alcohol is most popular with incoming freshmen, who seem to feel the need to abuse it once they get away from their parents. It stays a force throughout college life, especially once you and your friends start turning 21. Most of the time, your exposure to drugs at school depends on who you makes friends with. It's not hard to get sucked into a circle of potheads if you let it happen, but if you want to say no, you won't have a problem. Turning down alcohol at UM can be more difficult, as it plays an extremely important part in most students' social lives.

The College Prowler® Grade on

Drug Scene: B-

A high grade in the Drug Scene indicates that drugs are not a noticeable part of campus life; drug use is not visible, and no pressure to use them seems to exist.

Campus Strictness

The Lowdown On...
Campus Strictness

Students Are Most Likely to Get Caught...
Being publicly intoxicated
Burning candles or incense in dorm rooms
Downloading music on the school network
Drinking underage
Making too much noise in the dorms
Not leaving the room during fire alarms
Parking illegally or without a permit
Playing hallway sports
Setting off fire alarms
Smoking indoors
Stealing food from the dining halls

Students Speak Out On...
Campus Strictness

Q Not Strict
You can go wherever whenever, you can invite whoever (guy/girl) into your room whenever. Just don't play beer pong. Some Resident Assistance will write you up.

Q Pretty Much a Joke
Security doesn't do much... drinking and drug write-ups don't really mean anything... To me, that's an A+

Q Not That I Know of
I haven't seen any punishment because of how Peaceful it is.

Q Campus Strictness
Every floor has an RA that checks the floor every night with another RA, in order to make sure that kids are not partying and drinking or doing other illegal things in their rooms. If caught underage drinking, fines could be up to $175 dollars and loss of housing and/or suspension. Although it's pretty strict, our campus would be a mess without the university's policies.

Q Punishments Are Severe
Underage drinking, plagiarism and theft or any criminal activity is strictly enforced and punished. If you are going to partake in these activities, I would recommend you approach with caution and be very discrete.

Q RA DOOM
The RA's and the school are extremely strict on drug use and underage drinking. A fifth of my floor has been kicked

off the floor and almost everyone is on final probation. It is the farthest thing from a "red cup policy school" as you can get.

Q I guess they're strict, I've heard that our dorm had like 300 citations in the first two weeks of school. Oh, one of the frats got raided by the police the other day. They found drugs. Big surprise.

Q The campus police are not very strict. There are many spots where drug use is common knowledge but nothing is done.

The College Prowler Take On...
Campus Strictness

Students are quick to point out the presence of police officers on campus, especially late at night. This is a good thing as far as safety goes, but makes getting away with things a lot harder. Every floor of the residence halls has RAs who are trained to look out for drinking and other illicit activities. Some RAs are strict and will report you over anything, while others actually allow drinking as long as it doesn't get out of control. Either way, the RAs are usually pretty cool and are just trying to keep everyone safe. The campus police are strict, but they can't cover every corner of campus, so kids still get away with plenty of underage drinking, the most common infraction on campus. Students have to check in to the dorms whenever they return after 10 p.m., so if you come back totally drunk and unable to walk, you'll probably get written up for public intoxication. Normally the police won't be involved, but you'll have to meet with a counselor, and your parents will find out.

One of the more annoying areas of strictness is with the parking lot police. These guys ride around on golf carts and write tickets for anyone double parked or parked in the wrong lot, or even people who park over the white lines on the ground, even if the guy next to you was the cause of it. Some parking citations are absolutely ridiculous, but they're easy to appeal as long as you don't get too many. The most common reason for getting in trouble on campus is definitely underage drinking in the dorms. If you get noise complaints and run around the halls, even the most lenient RAs are bound to get fed up and turn you in.

The College Prowler® Grade on
Campus Strictness: C+

A high Campus Strictness grade implies an overall lenient atmosphere; police and RAs are fairly tolerant, and the administration's rules are flexible.

Parking

The Lowdown On...
Parking

Parking Services
Parking and Transportation
(305) 284-3096
parking@miami.edu
www.miami.edu/parking

Approximate Parking Permit Cost
$478 per year

Student Parking Lot
Yes

Freshmen Allowed to Park
No: Freshmen living on campus cannot have cars.

Common Parking Tickets

Expired meter: $20
Fire lane: $20, plus automatic towing and additional charges
Handicapped zone: $250
No parking zone: $20

Getting a Parking Permit

Permits are relatively easy to get if you apply within the first couple days of the year. You can apply on the school's network and the amount will be added to your bill automatically. You'll then have to go to the office in one of the garages on campus and pick up your permit, which hangs from your mirror and allows you access to almost all the lots on campus.

Did You Know?

Best Places to Find a Parking Spot
• Apartment area lot
• Ponce garage
• Pavia garage
• Mahoney/Pearson garage
• Bank United Center lot
• Anywhere on weekends and Friday or Saturday night

Good Luck Getting a Parking Spot Here!
• Hecht/Stanford lot
• School building and classroom lots (during the day)
• Mahoney/Pearson lot
• Eaton lot

Students Speak Out On...
Parking

Q Hurry Cane

Freshmen aren't allowed to have cars, but there are a few available spots if you are able to spend a lot of money. Otherwise parking is pretty easy to come by. Cars aren't necessary though, there is a good shuttle.

Q Sometimes a Nightmare

In order to find parking, one must arrive at least a half hour before class. Not to mention the permit costs.... astronomical!

Q Parking

Parking SUCKSSS and this is coming from a non-driver. You really do not need a car unless you commute but even then people use the metro and bus so yeah. You have to be willing to get to campus early for the best parking or you will end up walking further than needed to class.

Q It Sucks

Hard to find a spot, expensive, and ticketed way too easily. Freshman cannot have cars anymore so they're skrewed when it comes to getting off campus.

Q Good Luck Finding a Spot

Expect to pay about $350 for a parking permit for the year. On campus parking is expensive and hard to find. Tickets and fines run you from at least $20 to $50 or more; you can expect to get at least one during your academic career. Freshmen are no longer allowed to have cars on campus, so I have no idea what they do for fun since public transportation in Miami is a joke. They do have about three zip cars on campus to rent, but they're perpetually in use.

Q The parking scene is horrible. Most students on campus seem to have a car, and so parking spots are hard to come by. Parking on weekends is sometimes easier as many local students go home for the weekend.

Q Parking is crazy. Depending on where you live or where you want to park your car, it can be very difficult.

Q It seems that for an on-campus student, parking is not much of a problem. However, for commuter students, it is a severe issue. Either you will have to walk or take the shuttle from the garage and kill a bunch of time. Or you might have to park in the commuter lots and hope nothing happens to your car, such as scratches and dents.

The College Prowler Take On...
Parking

The good news about parking at UM is that decals are available for freshmen. The bad news is that Braveheart-like battle scenes erupt over every decent spot available. There are tons of spots in the lots and garages around campus, so if you can cover the ever-increasing cost of a decal, then you're guaranteed to find a place to park. But finding a spot within reasonable walking distance to your dorm is another story. The two dorms where most freshmen live share a long, narrow lot with most of the good spots reserved for RAs and other staff. If you get back to campus in the popular parking times, which seem to be almost always, then your only hope of getting anything in this lot is to beg strangers for their spots. Instead, you'll probably have to park at UM's basketball arena and drag your stuff down the street to the building you live in.

Other dorms on campus have similar parking problems. Finding a good spot is an accomplishment worthy of celebration, and whenever you do hit the parking lot jackpot, you'll be reluctant to move your car for days, or even weeks. Still, it's better to put up with the occasional long walk than to not be allowed to have a car at all as a freshman, a policy which is becoming popular among today's overcrowded schools. Miami is a great city, but without a car, you'll be stuck eating at the same few restaurants and going to same places around campus. If you bring a car to school, make sure to get your decal early, and try not to return to campus during weekday afternoons or mornings, when spots are rare. Evenings and weekends, when a lot of people leave campus, are the best times to find a place to park, but even then you should be prepared to walk.

The College Prowler® Grade on
Parking: C

A high grade in the Parking section indicates that parking is both available and affordable, and that parking enforcement isn't overly severe.

Transportation

The Lowdown On...
Transportation

Best Ways to Get Around Town
A bike (wear a helmet, this is Miami)
Your best friend's car
Hurry 'Cane Shuttle
Zip Cars

Campus Shuttle
Hurry 'Cane Shuttle
(305) 284-3096
Daily 7 a.m.–10 p.m.

Ibis Ride
(305) 284-3096
Friday–Saturday 8 p.m.–3:30 a.m.

RSMAS Shuttle
(305) 284-3096
Monday-Friday 7:45 a.m–5:30 p.m.

Sergeant Sebastian Escort
(305) 284-6666
Daily 6 p.m.–6 a.m.
After 12 a.m. by request

Public Transit

Metrorail

Elevated train system with a stop at UM

Best Ways to Get to the Airport

A cab ride to the airport costs $45.

Super Shuttle International (305) 871-2000 The van will pick you up in front of your dorm and take you to your terminal at MIA.

Nearest Airport

Miami International Airport

(305) 876-7000

The Miami International Airport is seven miles and approximately 20 minutes driving time from the University of Miami.

Nearest Passenger Bus

Miami Greyhound Bus Terminal

4111 NW 27th Street, Miami

(305) 871-1810

www.greyhound.com

The Greyhound Bus Station is near the Miami International Airport, approximately seven miles from campus.

Nearest Passenger Train

Miami Amtrak Train Station

8303 NW 37th Ave., Miami

800-872-7245

www.amtrak.com

The Amtrak Train Station is near Hialeah, approximately eight miles from campus.

Students Speak Out On...
Transportation

Q Buses Are Very Convenient

The school provides transportation to and from downtown
Miami, free to all students. There are shuttles to and from
the airports during vacation travel days. The subway of
Miami can sometimes be a hassle, but is great for a college
budget.

Q ZIP Cars

Public transportation is near by. They also have shuttle
buses to take you to the mall and cinemas. The Zip cars
are the best. You pay a yearly charge than you can rent by
the hour or day at a resonable charge.

Q Take Advantage

There are three shuttle loops that are run fairly well:1.
Runs loops to the grocery store and liquor store as well as
movie theater and shopping area (similar to an outdoor
mall.)2. Runs from the Greek houses and apartment areas
to class.3. Runs from the middle of campus (far from the
freshman dorms) to Coconut Grove (bar and restaurant
area) on Thursdays and maybe even Fridays and Saturdays.
(Drunk bus. Crazy stuff happens on these.)Metro stop a ten
minute walk off campus that can take you downtown or
next to a mall. 2$ each way. One stop connects to a train
that goes up and down South Florida (Miami to a little
north of Ft. Lauderdale.)Zip-cars are easy to find and use.
Not very cheap but better than a cab and good for when
you're in a crunch.Cabs are easy to get on most nights
but are very expensive. They are lenient on number in a
cab though. I've been in a normal sedan style cab with
the driver and six of my friends. Ended up being $1.50
a person.Knowing a friend with a car is very very helpful
and can be almost the most important thing during your

freshman year. The main reasons for needing a car are:1. Living off campus far away2. Living on campus and eating out on nights and weekends3. Shopping for stuff that's not available in malls or grocery stores.

Q It Works

The metro station is right across from campus. You can take it to the airports, South Beach, target, the mall, and a few other places. In general, the Miami transportation really isn't great, but it is doable. The school offers a shuttle that takes you down to the grove on Thursday and Fridays, Sunset mall,and the grocery store for free.

Q Hurry Canes

They have plenty of buses running on campus; the only problem is that they are really disorganized. They should send more buses around 15 minutes before a class starts, because there are a lot of people waiting then. They need to get a better Transportation Director. Also, the buses take students to places like Sunset Place, shopping, and Cocowalk on weekends sometimes. The administration is always trying to shut the weekend operations down because drunk kids get on the bus and throw up on occasion. What do you expect when you take a busload of kids out to the Grove?

Q No Parking Anywhere

There is no such thing as off campus parking and on campus parking costs a lot!

Q Awful Public Transportation

The city of Miami has terrible public transportation that is almost non-existent. The school however does provide their own shuttles to and from campus to places such as Coconut Grove, a place where young people go out to eat and shop. A car is very useful in Miami since everything is so far.

Q Public transportation is very convenient with the Metrorail located directly across the street from campus. Aside from that, school shuttles will take you to a lot of places on weekends, or you can just catch a cab.

The College Prowler Take On...
Transportation

The lack of efficient public transportation in Miami can't really be blamed on any specific thing. For one, Miami isn't set up like New York or Chicago, both cities whose metropolitan designs make it more convenient for trains and buses to get around. Since we're all living on heavily-paved swamp land down here, nothing can really be built underground. There are some semblances of public transportation, most notably the Metrorail, which is an elevated train system that runs from Medley, in northwest Miami-Dade, to Kendall. One of the stops of the Metrorail is across the street from the University of Miami, making it accessible to students. The downside of the Metrorail is that there are some sketchy Miami citizens riding the Metrorail. It would definitely be a good idea not to ride alone.

UM does its part to make transportation easier for students without cars. Recently, UM has offered bicycles to help its students get around. In an effort to be green, UM has also employed a Zip Car system that allows students to carpool and rent cars when they need them. The method students use most to get around is the free shuttle that takes you to grocery stores, shops, and movie theaters, as well as to various buildings around campus. Students are given rides by UM shuttles to the football games that are held in Dolphin Stadium. Most students don't really complain about the limited amount of public transportation. Instead they focus their time on borrowing their friends' cars or taking a free UM shuttle cleverly referred to as the Hurry 'Cane. Cabs aren't really widespread in Miami, but there are enough to get you home after a night of drinking or to take you to the airport, although most students prefer the cheaper Super Shuttle.

The College Prowler® Grade on
Transportation: B+

A high grade for Transportation indicates that campus buses, public buses, cabs, and rental cars are readily-available and affordable. Other determining factors include proximity to an airport and the necessity of transportation.

Weather

The Lowdown On...
Weather

Temperature Averages
Spring – High: 84 °F
Spring – Low: 68 °F
Summer – High: 91 °F
Summer – Low: 76 °F
Fall – High: 85 °F
Fall – Low: 72 °F
Winter – High: 77 °F
Winter – Low: 61 °F

Precipitation Averages
Spring: 3.81 in.
Summer: 7.65 in.
Fall: 6.00 in.
Winter: 2.04 in.

Students Speak Out On...
Weather

Q WEATHER IS GREAT
BECAUSE UNIV. OF MIAMI IS LOCATED IN MIAMI, FL, IT IS VERY WARM AND MOIST. GREAT OUTDOOR EXPERIENCE AND SO FORTH.

Q Sunny, Steamy and Beautiful.
Obviously UM has earned the name 'The Suntan U' for a reason! The hottest months of the year are May, August and September, but from October to April it's perfect weather (aside from the occasional storm). There's tons of outdoor seating available and the campus is green and always in bloom. The beach is close and the water is warm and clear. It's so beautiful here-- I'm born and raised in Florida and wouldn't live anywhere else!

Q Best
Weather is a little tricky because it rains out of nowhere but the best weather in the US.

Q I Love the Warmth.
Some students dislike how hot and humid Miami can get in the summer months, but I'm a summer person. It's nice that I no longer need snow boots in the winter. The fall and spring can bring in quite a few tropical storms, which makes it hard to stay dry when going from class to class.

Q It's Always Rainy in South Florida...
I rains constantly in Miami. Every year around the beginning of the fall semester there is always worries about hurricanes. Every season is rainy season. We never have to deal with cold weather though. When it doesn't rain the weather is beautiful.

Q Sunny South Florida

If you want to get away from the cold and the wet, Miami is the place to be. Even in the dead of "winter" students can still walk around in shorts and flip flops or work on their tan.

Q Amazing but Don't Be Fooled

The weather here is obviously very nice. What many people forget is that everyone vacations to Miami in the Spring and Winter.Fall: Very hot, very humid, and VERY rainy. You may think of the Suntan U when you think of Miami but do not be fooled about Fall weather here. It's unbearably hot if you're used to cool falls with Autumn leaves. I'm from Maryland and sweat buckets outside during August, September and October. It's uncomfortable and you'll appreciate the fact that everyone air conditions the crap out of everything. Expect RANDOM thunderstorms. By random, I mean that it will be sunny with blue skies and white clouds until early to mid afternoon and all of a sudden over a fifteen minute period it turns dark as can be and pours and lightnings for an hour or two. Pretty much every day... Temp: 70-95. Rain: Too Much. Humidity: 200%. Winter: Very comfortable. A main reason to choose Miami. This winter was uncharacteristically cold for a month where it almost snowed. Winter time usually entails weather from 55-80. On average: Sunny with blue skies and sun 3-4 days a week. Blue skies but barely any sun 1-2 days a week. Rain about one day a week for hours. Cloudy and cool 1-2 days a week. Humidity is much more minimal than fall and isn't noticeable.Spring: Early spring is classic Miami weather. 70's and 80's and sunny with a few thunderstorms. Can be in the 60's and 90's but it's pretty relaxing. Humidity is a little noticeable but nothing terrible.

Q Rains a Lot

The University is a very opened-air campus. When it rains in Miami, it rains hard. This makes going to classes during raining season quite a challenge.

The College Prowler Take On...
Weather

Bring lots of heavy coats and sweatpants, You won't wear them, but you can always sell them on eBay for extra spending money during the semester, The unofficial University of Miami uniform for guys is basically cargo shorts, sandals, a hat or visor, and a T-shirt from an overrated band or beer company, Girls' tastes are, of course, more eclectic, but a typical wardrobe would be made up mostly of jeans, shorts, tank tops, and T-shirts, along with a few nice outfits for going out at night, Most students also suggest bringing umbrellas and rain ponchos, but you'll probably forget these in your room most of the time anyway,

The weather in Miami is beautiful throughout most of the year, but as soon as it dips below 70, people bring out the hooded sweatshirts and jeans, Students who grew up with snow and hail are reduced to shivering in between sips of steaming hot coffee after living in Miami for only a few months, But even on the coldest days of the year, when the temperature might drop into the high 40s, students refuse to lose the sandals, as if they're taking some kind of stand against the bitter cold, The biggest negative about Miami's weather is that there are always threats of hurricanes every season, Sometimes, there may be more than one hurricane heading toward South Florida! Despite the recent surge in watches and warnings, Miami has sustained very little damage, The University is very prepared for these storms, Hurricanes can be a good thing, especially if school is canceled because of an approaching storm, If a direct storm does directly hit UM, despite the precautions taken, serious damage could occur, In daily life, though, the only problem with the weather in South Florida is the unpredictable showers and the stifling heat... For the rest of this editorial, visit collegeprowler.com.

A

The College Prowler® Grade on
Weather: A

A high Weather grade designates that temperatures are mild and rarely reach extremes, that the campus tends to be sunny rather than rainy, and that weather is fairly consistent rather than unpredictable.

Report Card Summary

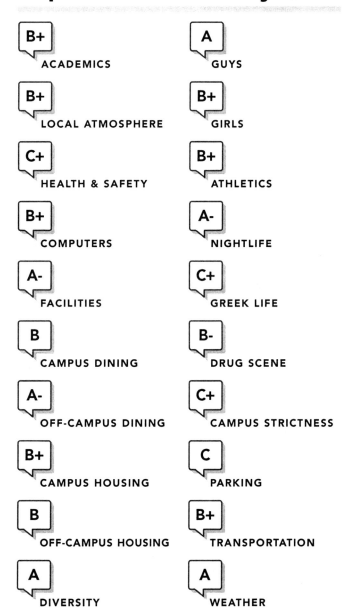

B+
ACADEMICS

A
GUYS

B+
LOCAL ATMOSPHERE

B+
GIRLS

C+
HEALTH & SAFETY

B+
ATHLETICS

B+
COMPUTERS

A-
NIGHTLIFE

A-
FACILITIES

C+
GREEK LIFE

B
CAMPUS DINING

B-
DRUG SCENE

A-
OFF-CAMPUS DINING

C+
CAMPUS STRICTNESS

B+
CAMPUS HOUSING

C
PARKING

B
OFF-CAMPUS HOUSING

B+
TRANSPORTATION

A
DIVERSITY

A
WEATHER

Overall Experience

Students Speak Out On...
Overall Experience

Q Student Opportunities

The University of Miami is high cost academic institution, but the sacrifice pays off incredibly. That money that students is received back tenfold in value if you take advantage of the events and activities availables to students. The school budgets provides so many leadership, social, cultural, and volunteer opportunites, with free transportation included.

Q Best Choice

This was the best decision I have ever made. Coming to UM is like a dream come true. You do not have to be rich, drunk, or high all the time to fit in. There is so much diversity on campus that you will find your niche. Whether it is a club, sport, or greek organization there is bound to be something for you. Yeah there are parties and stuff but majority of the people here work hard everyday and it shows, that is why we are #50!

Q Better Education

UM challenges your mind and there is always at least one teacher who wants to see you excel. It is a school where you will have fun and learn about other things and people outside of your everyday groups.

Q Stick With It.

Hated it first semester, was 99.9% sure I was going to transfer.I'm loving second semester. Better classes, now pledging a fraternity which stands for something and is a blast to be in.If you find you're niche, you'll have a great time. If not, you'll be miserable and want to get the hell out.

Q Love UM Hate Miami

The campus is really pretty, and of course you can't find fault with the weather. I just miss the Northeast and wish I had gone to a more college-y town for school. Miami is pretty urban, but not in the same way as places like Chicago or Boston, it's also really expensive. I love Miami as a place to vacation, but living here is very stressful and at times unpleasant

Q So Far

I just transferred here so all I can say is that the professors are great, the campus is beautiful and the students are very nice and sociable.

Q

I love it! I just had a great time last night partying with my sorority sisters and frat boys!

Q I really like this school a lot. There are times when I wish I was back with my friends at home, and sometimes I think that the girls are looking for the perfect hard body, which really sucks. But I have plenty of friends, and the school is great.

The College Prowler Take On...
Overall Experience

Despite daily griping about tuition costs, parking, thunderstorms, and hard classes, most students really seem to enjoy UM. Excellent attributes like the nightlife, weather, and culture seem to cancel out some of the bad things about being in Miami. For some students, these bad things include the unapproachable "hot" girls and guys on campus, while others find life in the dorms to be a challenge. The complaints about college are basically what you'd expect to hear anywhere. It appears that the bad things at UM really aren't that bad, but the good things are very good. Miami is one of the coolest cities in the world for a college student, and that goes deeper than just the superficial bar and club scene.

Students who are unhappy generally figure it out within a semester and transfer out of UM, usually to somewhere closer to home. College is tough, especially the first couple weeks if you come without knowing anyone. Making a whole new group of friends for the first time since kindergarten is one of the hardest and most stressful things you may ever have to do. But the end result of this process is friendships that you'll likely maintain for the rest of your life. Whether it's your roommate, classmates, fraternity brother, or sorority sister, college is a time when you should make friends and have fun. Despite the initial challenges of coming to college, there are few cities in the world that are as fun as Miami.

The Inside Scoop

The Lowdown On...
The Inside Scoop

School Slang

8-Care: Dial this on your room phone whenever the power goes out, the air conditioning breaks, or anything else goes wrong with school equipment, and a UM employee will come fix it.

Book Horizons: The sketchy bookstore across the street from campus that sometimes gets books cheaper than its on-campus rival; also carries school supplies and UM merchandise.

Chartwells: The name of the two dining halls on campus, also known to disgruntled students as Chart-Hells.

The C-Store: The convenience store located in the UC, which stays open until the middle of the night and accepts dining dollars.

Dining Dollars: Money that comes with a student's meal plan, which can be used like a credit card at most of the restaurants on campus.

Hurricane Drive: The street that runs through campus, past the baseball field and the fraternity houses; connects Ponce to the back roads of the campus; also known as San Amaro Drive.

The IM Field: A giant field that is used for intramurals or just for fun.

The Lake: Lake Osceola, a huge body of water in the center of campus; a path around it connects the Towers to Eaton Residential College, the UC, and several campus buildings.

The LC: The Whitten Learning Center, a group of lecture-sized classrooms where many large classes are held.

Memorial: A long building that holds hundreds of classes per day, as well as the campus movie theater.

Metrorail: Miami's elevated train system

myUM: The name of the computer network where students can log in to retrieve their grades, professor rankings, course schedules, and most other student-related information.

The Pit: A large, mysterious hole in the ground behind Memorial where students study and hang out under the cover of thick trees.

Ponce: The smaller road running right past campus, which runs through downtown Coral Gables. Real name: Ponce de Leon Blvd.

The Rat: Refers to the Rathskeller, a popular bar on campus.

Resident Master: A member of the faculty who lives in an apartment in the lobby of every residential college; the teacher and his or her family act as a host for the students living in the building and often have students over for dinner or meetings.

The Rock: The main area outside of the UC where pep rallies, protests, and other campus events are held.

Sebastian the Ibis: The school's mascot, a common face around campus; the ibis is supposedly the last bird to leave before a hurricane and the first to return afterwards.

Stanford Circle: The driveway outside the UC where students get picked up and dropped off; the name refers to Stanford Drive, which is the main entrance to the campus.

The Towers: The dorms where most freshmen live, also known as Hecht and Stanford; there are actually two 12-story buildings in each dorm, making for four identical "towers" on one side of the lake.

U.S. 1: The main road running near campus that is almost always insanely crowded; this road runs from Key West up to Maine, where the traffic must ease up slightly.

The UC: The University Center, aptly located in the center of campus, which is home to the food court, a student lounge, the book store, a swimming pool, and assorted offices.

Unicco: The janitorial service on campus that cleans the floor bathrooms, halls, and study lounges; treat the Unicco staff nicely or they may not get to your floor's bathroom for a while.

Things I Wish I Knew Before Coming To School

• According to University policy a student does not have to have more than two finals per day.

• An up-to-date video game system will make you plenty of friends in a hurry.

• Bring a long Ethernet cord so you can use your laptop in bed.

• Bring plenty of quarters to wash clothes, because, for some reason, there are no change machines in the laundry rooms.

• Don't buy the posters they sell on campus in the first couple weeks. Prices plummet later in the semester when they're desperate to get rid of inventory.

• Get the smallest meal plan allowed.

• If you're a light sleeper, bring earplugs, because the freshman dorms are usually pretty loud late into the night.

• Leave your door open for the first week so people on the floor feel like they can talk to you. Walk around to others' rooms and talk to them.

• Make friends with people in your orientation group, especially ones of the opposite sex.

• Never buy school merchandise (clothes and hats) from the bookstore on campus, unless you like long lines and inflated prices.

• Some local restaurants offer UM student's discounts.

• Students can get their clothes dry-cleaned in the UC.

• Students can sell back their books to the UM bookstore all year round.

• The air conditioners don't always do what you want, so be

prepared to make wardrobe or linen adjustments.
• The second floor of the Student Health Center has a student pharmacy.

Tips to Succeed

• Don't get too involved in campus activities unless you're confident in your grades and ability to study.
• Enjoy your major, or you'll hate it here.
• Find people on your floor that have the same classes or major as you and share notes.
• Free tutoring is offered at the Academic Development center for those students who need it.
• Get used to using a computer for everything. There are plenty of classes that are very research based, and hand-written assignments are rarely accepted anymore.
• Go to your classes!
• Look up student evaluations of professors on my UM or check out ratemyprofessor.com before you choose your classes.
• Party responsibly and exhibit self control. Do not stay up partying all night, all of the time limit it to the weekends.
• Pay attention to your advisers during orientation, especially when they talk about student life.
• Pick an academic adviser early and make sure he or she knows who you are and what your interests are.
• Sit in the front of the class and make sure the professor knows your name if you actually want to get something out of the course.
• Stay on top of deadlines.
• Study rooms in the library can be reserved in advance
• Talk to your professors. This is the number one piece of advice.

Traditions

Boat-Burning Ceremony: This tradition takes place during homecoming and involves burning a boat on Lake Osceola. Fireworks conclude this exciting event.
The Breezeway : This is a tunnel that splits the UC in half, and is the site of a frenzied stockmarket-like atmosphere

on weekday afternoons. The short, narrow walkway is full of students coming to and from classes, and so organizations set up tables to try to sell stuff or promote themselves. This can be a good thing if you're looking for weird antiques or girl scout cookies, and it does allow for some groups to get their name out, but overall it seems like a nuisance to most students.

Homecoming : This is not an event exclusive to UM, but some of the events happening during the week are pretty unique. For example, the school always gets an old car and writes the name of the team we play in football that weekend. Students then line up to take out their aggression on the car, sledgehammer-style.

Hurricane Howl: The Hurricane Howl is a pep rally that starts the Homecoming festivities. After attending the sprit-filled pep rally, students can enjoy a concert on the UC patio.

Hurricanes Help the Hometown : This is one of many service-oriented events taking place every year. For this, students dedicate a Saturday morning and afternoon to volunteering at dozens of locations all through Miami. Many of the participants are there from fraternities and sororities, since the event is part of Homecoming, but others come out just to help the community in any way they can.

Iron Arrow : This is the University's oldest and most mysterious tradition. The true inner workings of this honor society are only available to its members, who are hand picked every semester. Membership is extremely limited and competitive, but members swear that this Seminole Indian-influenced organization has changed who they are.

Miss UM Pageant: This annual event showcases many beautiful women competing for the title and crown of Miss UM.

President's Picnic: Before the beginning of every fall semester, President Shalala invites all students to her house in Coral Gables for a lunch. Buses take students to the house, where they are able to mingle with the president and other administrators. This event includes fabulous food and a great deal of Cane Spirit.

Sportsfest : This is a yearly competition where residential colleges battle one another in various sporting events. The dorms, broken up by floor, field teams to compete in games ranging from football to rock, paper, scissors. The winner is declared Sportsfest champion and gets a trophy on display in the Wellness Center.

Urban Legends

• A lone crocodile makes its home in the lake on campus, where it sometimes feeds on fish in front of awed students. There are also rumors that the crocodile was removed by wildlife officials.

• A student drowned in the lake a couple years ago after taking a swim during a hurricane.

• Football players and other athletes go to the dining halls for steaks and huge portions of food not available to regular students.

• To the delight of the male student body, the Olsen twins were considering UM before settling on another school.

Students Speak Out On...
The Inside Scoop

Q Tan at the Beach?

If you go to UM, you can always go to the pool or the beach right after you are done with classes. It's basically summer throughout the year. A lot of students wear bathing suits under dresses to class. There are many good malls around, so you can go there when you are bored. To South Beach, it takes only 20 minutes to get there! Everyone at this school cares about both academics and parties, so if you think you can balance it out, then come to the UM :D!

Q Pep Rallys

During football season, my school knows how to pump up the crowd. We hold a pep rally every home game, and at the beginning of the season, my school sells shirts for $2 to the student body so we may be able to support our school during the games.

Q Why UM?

The University of Miami is currently ranked number 1 academically in the state of FL, and has one of the best football programs. The U invented swager. The weather is always beautiful - great choice for Undergrad. The Beach is 10 minutes away (btw, a great place to study). Students here know how to work hard and play hard. There's a big party scene, but we remember to keep GPA's high enough to keep scholarships. UM is one of the best choices I've made.

Q Insider

The community is very diverse and it is very fun to be around other people. Every body is very accepting and there's guys for every taste :p

Q All-Around Awesome

UM is really the best of every world for a perspective college student. The academics are renowned, the music school is top notch, the room and food options are diverse and high-quality, and the social scene/college experience is what every high school senior dreams of.

Q Nothing Is Perfect

If you come to this school thinking that all the parties and social life activities will be on or near campus you will be disappointed. 98% of social life happens off campus, people go to the grove, south beach and off campus house parties to get their drink on. Because of this a car is almost a necessity, the public transportation is very pathetic only useful if you want to go to downtown but the metro rail stops at 12am and most people dont even leave for a club by then so it is useless at night. Also the name University of Miami is very misleading do to the fact that the actual city is about 15 mins away so it isnt quite city life but a more quite suburban atmosphere (on campus concerts must be shut down before 12am or else coral gables police will shut them down). Aside from those things the school is beautiful and has pull throughout the nation not just Florida and is ideal for almost any major. Also the weather is unbeatable, if you want a school that almost has it all, because lets face it every school has draw backs, you should really look into this school.

Q Different from My Expectations

Girls are more fake than I thought.Frats are not all complete drunken messes.Much more of a commuter campus than I thought.Classes can be great or horrible.

Not much in-between.Find somewhere to go to house parties if you like them, because they're not that easy to find.

Jobs & Internships

The Lowdown On...
Jobs & Internships

Employment Services?
Yes

Placement Services?
Yes

Other Career Services
CaneTRAK
Career Column
Career Development Series
Career Exploration Week
Discover

Power Networking
Toppel Career Library
Vault

Advice

The Toppel Career Center is a great resource for students thinking ahead. There are numerous conventions on campus every year where hundreds of potential employers come to collect résumés or talk to students about job opportunities. As far as internships go, most individual schools within the University have a staff member to talk to students about internships during their stay at UM. Get to know your school's internship adviser so that he or she comes to you first with the best offers. If you're looking to get started on internships early, talk to older students in your major to see if they can recommend something for you. Later on in your college career, head over to the Toppel Career Center and meet with someone there to discuss future job offers.

Alumni & Post-Grads

The Lowdown On...
Alumni & Post-Grads

Alumni Office
Office of Alumni Relations
1550 Brescia Ave., Coral
Gables
Phone: (305) 284-2872
alumni@miami.edu
www.miami.edu/alumni

Major Alumni Events
Major alumni events include
Homecoming, the Alumni
Association Awards Program,
class reunions, football
games, and the Alumni Golf
Tour.

Services Available
Access to tickets for UM
sporting events
Campus parking pass
Entry to UM facilities like the
library and Wellness Center
Transcript services for
members of the Alumni
Association

Alumni Publications
Miami Magazine is published
every semester and is
included as a benefit of
joining the University of

Miami Alumni Association, which requires an annual contribution to maintain membership.

Did You Know?

Famous UM Alums:
Rick Berry (Class of '65) - basketball Hall-of-Fame member
Gloria Estefan (Class of '78) - singer/entertainer
Roy Firestone (Class of '75) - TV personality and former ESPN host
Jerry Herman (Class of '53) - Emmy-nominated musician and composer
Bruce Hornsby (Class of '77) - singer/musician
Patricia Ireland (Class of '75) - former National Organization for Women (NOW) president
Dwayne Johnson (Class of '95) - professional wrestler and actor, known as "The Rock"
Suzy Kolber (Class of '86) - sideline reporter for ESPN
Al Rosen (Class of '48) - former president of the Houston Astros baseball team
Sylvester Stallone (Class of '99) - Academy Award-nominated writer/actor for Rocky

Student Organizations

The Lowdown On...

ROTC
Air Force ROTC: Yes
Navy ROTC: No
Army ROTC: Yes

Student Activities Offered

Ad Group – students interested in advertising

Adrian Empire – Medieval Times appreciation group www.adrianempire.org/

African Students Union – www.miami.edu/studorgs/asu/

Aikido Club – www.miami.edu/studorgs/aikido/

Alpha Epsilon Delta – pre-med honor society www.aedmiami.org/

Alpha Eta Mu Beta – biomedical engineering honor society

Alpha Kappa Psi – business club. www.umakpsi.com/

Alpha Mu Music Theory Club

Alternative Spring Break

American Association of Pre-Dental Students

American Institute of Aeronautics and Astronautics

American Institute of Architecture Students

American Medical Student Association, Premedical Chapter – www.amsa.go.to/

American Society of Civil Engineers

American Society of Mechanical Engineers – www.eng.miami.edu/~umasme/

Amnesty International – UM chapter of a group promoting human rights

Animal Allies – www.miami.

edu/studorgs/hha/

Anthropology Club

Architectural Engineering Institute

Asian American Students Association – www.miami.edu/studorgs/aasa/

The Associate Members of Lambda Sigma Upsilon – a Latino fraternity promoting educational and social experiences – www.lsu79.org/index_shield.html

Association for Computing Machinery – www.acm.miami.edu/

Association of Commuter Students – www.miami.edu/studorgs/acs/

Association of Cuban-American Engineers – coeds.eng.miami.edu/~umace/

Association of Greek Letter Organizations

Association of Officials and Event Specialists

Athletes in Action – looks at religion in sports -www.athletesinaction.org/

AWARE! – promotes awareness of AIDS

BACCHUS – promotes responsible consumption of alcohol- www.miami.edu/studorgs/bacchus/

Badminton – www.miami.edu/wellness-clubs/badminton/

Baptist College Ministries

– www.miami.edu/studorgs/
bcm/
Best Buddies – www.miami.
edu/studorgs/bestbuddies/
Beta Beta Beta – a group of
students interested in natural
science
Bioethics Society – www.
miami.edu/studorgs/
bioethics/
Biomedical Engineering
Society – www.eng.miami.
edu/~umbmes/
Black Filmmakers Association
Black Nursing Student
Association
Bowling Club
Brothers Overcoming
Negativity and Destruction
Campus Advent – allows
students to meet others with
an interest in the Seventh-day
Adventist denomination
Campus Colors – a magazine
supporting diversity on
campus
Campus Crusade for Christ –
www.godsquad.com/
Canes for Cancer Awareness
Canes Kids – www.wementor.
org/
Caribbean Students
Association – www.miami.
edu/studorgs/coiso/
Catholics Students
Association – www.saintau-
gustinechurch.org/
Chi Alpha Christian
Fellowship – www.miami.edu/
studorgs/chialpha/

Circle K International –
provides experience in group
participation
Colombian Student
Association
Committee on Student
Organizations – www.miami.
edu/coso/
Council of International
Students and Organizations
– www.miami.edu/studorgs/
coiso/
Cricket Club
Criminal Justice Club
Dancing Ibis – salsa dancing
club – groups.yahoo.com/
group/universityofmiamis-
alsa/
Delta Sigma Pi – supports the
study of business and
commercial ethics
Earth Alert
Elections Commission – www.
miami.edu/student-activities/
Engineering Advisory Board
– www.eng.miami.
edu/~umeab/
Entrepreneurship Board –
applies classroom business
lessons to the real world
Episcopal Students
Organization
Equestrian Club – www.
miami.edu/studorgs/umet/
Federacion de Estudiantes
Cubanos – promotes
awareness of Cuban culture
Fencing Club
Filipino Student Association
– www.miami.edu/studorgs/

fsa/
Florida Collegiate Music
Educators National
Conference
French Club
Friendship Club of China
– phyvax.ir.miami.edu:8001/
fcc/index2.html
FunDay – helps plan a day of
friendship between UM
students and people with
mental disabilities
Generation-X Entrepreneur
Club
Geological and
Environmental Outings
German Club
Golden Key International
Honour Society – www.
miami.edu/studorgs/
golden-key/
Golf Club – www.miami.edu/
wellness/club/
Habitat for Humanity
Haitian Students
Organization
Hindu Students Council –
www.miami.edu/studorgs/
hsc/
Hip-Hop Club – www.
umhiphopclub.com/
Hispanic Heritage Month
Association
History Club
Homecoming Executive
Committee – www.miami.
edu/homecoming/
Honor Students' Association
– hsa.go.to/
Hui Aloha – promotes

awareness of Hawaiian
culture
Hurricane Productions – an
entertainment-planning
committee for campus
events. www.miami.edu/
hurricane-productions/
Ibis – students create and
produce all aspects of the
yearbook
Indian Students Association
– www.um-isa.org/
Inquiry: The Research
Connection – encourages
students' interests in research
Institute of Industrial
Engineers – www.eng.miami.
edu/~umiie/
InterFraternity Council –
www.miami.edu/studorgs/ifc/
InterVarsity Christian
Fellowship
Islamic Society
Italian Club – umitalianclub.
tripod.com/
Jewish Student Organization
KAOS – allows students to
choreograph and perform
hip-hop dances
Karate Club
Latin America Student
Association
Latino Greek Council
Latter-Day Saints Student
Association
LINK – promotes leadership
through volunteer events –
www.miami.edu/studorgs/
link/
Marine Mammal Stranding

Team – helps rescue stranded marine mammals.

Men's Soccer Club – www.miami.edu/wellness/club/

Miami Hurrican – Student Paper (twice weekly)

Microbiology and Immunology Club – www.miami.edu/studorgs/microbiology/

Minority Association of Pre-Health Students

Mortar Board National Honor Society

Music and Entertainment Industry Student Association – www.miami.edu/studorgs/meisa/

Muslim Students Organization – www.miami.edu/studorgs/mso/

National Association of Black Accountants – www.nabainc.org/pages/Home.jsp

National Broadcasting Society – www.miami.edu/studorgs/nbs/

National Pan-Hellenic Council – governs the historically African American fraternities and sororities

National Society of Black Engineers – www.eng.miami.edu/~umnsbe/

National Society of Collegiate Scholars

OASIS – promotes Arab culture and history

Omicron Delta Kappa – a society for outstanding leaders on campus – www.miami.edu/studorgs/odk/

Organization for Jamaican Unity – www.miami.edu/studorgs/oju/

Panhellenic Association – governs the historically white sororities

Phi Alpha Delta, Pre-Legal Society – www.miami.edu/studorgs/pad/

Phi Sigma Pi National Leadership Fraternity

Phi Sigma Tau – an honor society for philosophy students – www.miami.edu/phi/phisigmatau/

Philosophy Club – www.miami.edu/phi/phiclub/

Project Sunshine – volunteers to help sick children at Miami Children's Hospital – www.projectsunshine.org/

Promoting Health Awareness Through Education – www.miami.edu/wellness/club/

Psi Chi – organization for students of psychology – www.miami.edu/studorgs/psi-chi/

Public Relations Student Society of America

QuantUM Entertainment – promotes the creation of student-produced entertainment – www.gotoquantum.com/

Racquetball Club

Roller Hockey Club – www.miami.edu/wellness-clubs/

roller_hockey/

Rowing Club

Rugby Club – www.miami.
edu/wellness/club/

Sailing Hurricanes – www.
miami.edu/wellness-clubs/
sailing/

Scandinavian Student
Association

School of Architecture
Student Council

Scuba Club – www.miami.
edu/wellness/club/

Self-Experiencing Through
Volunteering and Altruism

Society for the Study of
Religions and Cultures –
www.miami.edu/studorgs/
ssrc/

Society of Hispanic
Professional Engineers –
www.eng.miami.
edu/~umshpe/

Society of Manufacturing
Engineers

Society of Women Engineers
– www.eng.miami.
edu/~umswe/

Solutions – allows students
and faculty to informally
discuss issues

SpectrUM – supports the
acceptance of the gay,
lesbian, and bisexual
community – www.miami.
edu/studorgs/spectrum/

Sport and Recreational
Interest Clubs Federation

Squash Club

Strictly Business Association

Student Activity Fee
Allocation Committee – www.
miami.edu/safac/

Student Government

Student Health Advisory
Committee

Students for a Free Tibet

Students Together Ending
Poverty

Surfrider Club

Swimming and Aquatics Club

Table Tennis Club

Tae Kwon Do Club – www.
miami.edu/wellness-clubs/
taekwondo/

Technology Management
Association

Tennis Club

Trinidad and Tobago Cultural
Association – www.math.
miami.edu/~ttca/tt.html

Ultimate Frisbee Club

United Black Students – www.
miami.edu/studorgs/ubs/

United Dominicans
Association – www.miami.
edu/studorgs/uda/

University of Miami American
Red Cross

University of Miami Baseball
Club

University of Miami
Filmmakers Association

University of Miami Lacrosse
Club

University of Miami
Percussion Club

University of Miami Young
Democrats

Virgin Islands Student

Association
Volleyball Club – www.miami.
edu/wellness-clubs/
volleyball/
A Week for Life – educates
the community about HIV/
AIDS
Wesley Foundation –
promotes Christian
leadership – www.miami.edu/
wesley/
William R. Butler Inspiration
Concert Choir
Women in Business
Women's Fastpitch Softball
Club
Women's Resource Center
Programming Board – www.
miami.edu/womens-center/
Women's Soccer Club – www.
miami.edu/wellness/club/
WVUM – campus radio
station – www.wvum.org/
Yanxin Qigong Club –
practices traditional Chinese
meditation
Yellow Rose Society –
promotes awareness of
female issues -groups.msn.
com/yellowrosesociety/_
homepage

The Best

The **BEST** Things

1. Sports teams

2. Hot guys and girls

3. Local clubs and bars - Miami has great nightlife, and some bars and clubs don't close until 4 a.m.

4. Walking around in December in sandals

5. Local culture (Little Havana and South Beach)

6. Great off-campus restaurants

7. Arranging classes so that you have Mondays, Wednesdays, and Fridays off

8. Walking past a lake and palm trees on the way to class every day

9. Diversity

10. Miami's 24-hour culture

The Worst

The **WORST** Things

1. The traffic everywhere in Miami

2. When tropical storms and hurricanes cause several straight days of rain

3. Parking availability close to the dorms

4. Dining halls

5. Dorms with shared bathrooms

6. Struggling to understand Spanish and Spanish accents around Miami

7. The packed Metrorail ride to the Orange Bowl on game days

8. High tuition costs

9. Snobby people

10. Long distances between buildings

Visiting

The Lowdown On...
Visiting

Campus Tours

Campus tours leave during the school year every weekday at 11 a.m., 1:30 p.m., and 3 p.m. from the Office of Undergraduate Admission. Saturday tours start at 10:30 a.m., and information sessions are available by appointment. Weekday tours during the summer leave at 11 a.m. All tours last approximately one hour and are led by current UM students.

Virtual Tour of Campus

www.miami.edu/interactive-tour

Interviews & Information Sessions

Call (305) 284-4323 to confirm the availability of an information session or come to the Office of Undergraduate Admission on any weekday at 12:30 p.m. Admissions officers hold information sessions at 12:30 p.m. every Monday-Friday at the Office of Undergraduate Admission on campus. This office is located in the Bowman Foster Ashe building. Check with the office at the number above to confirm that a session will be held on the day of your visit. Reservations are not required.

Overnight Visits

While the school does not offer any overnight programs, it would be a great experience to spend a night in the dorms with a current UM student. Check with any friends you may have at UM to see if they'll let you stay for a night, or as a last resort, contact your high school's guidance office about past students who have gone to UM. Be careful when you come though. Every night of the week isn't like Saturday, even in party-happy Miami. Likewise, a Monday night might be more boring than a Thursday.

Words to Know

Academic Probation – A suspension imposed on a student if he or she fails to keep up with the school's minimum academic requirements. Those unable to improve their grades after receiving this warning can face dismissal.

Beer Pong/Beirut – A drinking game involving cups of beer arranged in a pyramid shape on each side of a table. The goal is to get a ping pong ball into one of the opponent's cups by throwing the ball or hitting it with a paddle. If the ball lands in a cup, the opponent is required to drink the beer.

Bid – An invitation from a fraternity or sorority to 'pledge' (join) that specific house.

Blue-Light Phone – Brightly-colored phone posts with a blue light bulb on top. These phones exist for security purposes and are located at various outside locations around most campuses. In an emergency, a student can pick up one of these phones (free of charge) to connect with campus police or a security escort.

Campus Police – Police who are specifically assigned to a given institution. Campus police are typically not regular city officers; they are employed by the university in a full-time capacity.

Club Sports – A level of sports that falls somewhere between varsity and intramural. If a student is unable to commit to a varsity team but has a lot of passion for athletics, a club sport could be a better, less intense option. Even less demanding, intramural (IM) sports often involve no traveling and considerably less time.

Cocaine – An illegal drug. Also known as "coke" or "blow," cocaine often resembles a white crystalline or powdery substance. It is highly addictive and dangerous.

Common Application – An application with which students can apply to multiple schools.

Course Registration – The period of official class selection for the upcoming quarter or semester. Prior to registration, it is best to prepare several back-up courses in case a particular class becomes full. If a course is full, students can place themselves on the waitlist, although this still does not guarantee entry.

Division Athletics – Athletic classifications range from Division I to Division III. Division IA is the most competitive, while Division III is considered to be the least competitive.

Dorm – A dorm (or dormitory) is an on-campus housing facility. Dorms can provide a range of options from suite-style rooms to more communal options that include shared bathrooms. Most first-year students live in dorms. Some upperclassmen who wish to stay on campus also choose this option.

Early Action – An application option with which a student can apply to a school and receive an early acceptance response without a binding commitment. This system is becoming less and less available.

Early Decision – An application option that students should use only if they are certain they plan to attend the school in question. If a student applies using the early decision option and is admitted, he or she is required and bound to attend that university. Admission rates are usually higher among students who apply through early decision, as the student is clearly indicating that the school is his or her first choice.

Ecstasy – An illegal drug. Also known as "E" or "X," ecstasy looks like a pill and most resembles an aspirin. Considered a party drug, ecstasy is very dangerous and can be deadly.

Ethernet – An extremely fast Internet connection available in most university-owned residence halls. To use an Ethernet connection properly, a student will need a network card and cable for his or her computer.

Fake ID – A counterfeit identification card that contains false information. Most commonly, students get fake IDs with altered birthdates so that they appear to be older than 21 (and therefore of legal drinking age). Even though it is illegal, many college students have fake IDs in hopes of purchasing alcohol or getting into bars.

Frosh – Slang for "freshman" or "freshmen."

Hazing – Initiation rituals administered by some fraternities or sororities as part of the pledging process. Many universities have outlawed hazing due to its degrading, and sometimes dangerous, nature.

Intramurals (IMs) – A popular, and usually free, sport league in which students create teams and compete against one another. These sports vary in competitiveness and can include a range of activities—everything from billiards to water polo. IM sports are a great way to meet people with similar interests.

Keg – Officially called a half-barrel, a keg contains roughly 200 12-ounce servings of beer.

LSD – An illegal drug, also known as acid, this hallucinogenic drug most commonly resembles a tab of paper.

Marijuana – An illegal drug, also known as weed or pot; along with alcohol, marijuana is one of the most commonly found drugs on campuses across the country.

Major –The focal point of a student's college studies; a specific topic that is studied for a degree. Examples of majors include physics, English, history, computer science, economics, business, and music. Many students decide on a specific major before arriving on campus, while others are simply "undecided" until declaring a major. Those who are extremely interested in two areas can also choose to double major.

Meal Block – The equivalent of one meal. Students on a meal plan usually receive a fixed number of meals per week. Each meal, or "block," can be redeemed at the school's dining facilities in place of cash. Often, a student's weekly allotment of meal blocks will be forfeited if not used.

Minor – An additional focal point in a student's education. Often serving as a complement or addition to a student's main area of focus, a minor has fewer requirements and prerequisites to fulfill than a major. Minors are not required for graduation from most schools; however some students who want to explore many different interests choose to pursue both a major and a minor.

Mushrooms – An illegal drug. Also known as "'shrooms," this drug resembles regular mushrooms but is extremely hallucinogenic.

Off-Campus Housing – Housing from a particular landlord or rental group that is not affiliated with the university. Depending on the college, off-campus housing can range from extremely popular to non-existent. Students who choose to live off campus are typically given more freedom, but they also have to deal with possible subletting scenarios, furniture, bills, and other issues. In addition to these factors, rental prices and distance often affect a student's decision to move off campus.

Office Hours – Time that teachers set aside for students who have questions about coursework. Office hours are a good forum for students to go over any problems and to show interest in the subject material.

Pledging – The early phase of joining a fraternity or sorority, pledging takes place after a student has gone through rush and received a bid. Pledging usually lasts between one and two semesters. Once the pledging period is complete and a particular student has done everything that is required to become a member, that student is considered a brother or sister. If a fraternity or a sorority would decide to "haze" a group of students, this initiation would take place during the pledging period.

Private Institution – A school that does not use tax revenue to subsidize education costs. Private schools typically cost more than public schools and are usually smaller.

Prof – Slang for "professor."

Public Institution – A school that uses tax revenue to subsidize education costs. Public schools are often a good value for in-state residents and tend to be larger than most private colleges.

Quarter System (or Trimester System) – A type of academic calendar system. In this setup, students take classes for three academic periods. The first quarter usually starts in late September or early October and concludes right before Christmas. The second quarter usually starts around early to mid–January and finishes up around March or April. The last academic quarter, or "third quarter," usually starts in late March or early April and finishes up in late May or Mid-June. The fourth quarter is summer. The major difference between the quarter system and semester system is that students take more, less comprehensive courses under the quarter calendar.

RA (Resident Assistant) – A student leader who is assigned to a particular floor in a dormitory in order to help to the other students who live there. An RA's duties include ensuring student safety and providing assistance wherever possible.

Recitation – An extension of a specific course; a review session. Some classes, particularly large lectures, are supplemented with mandatory recitation sessions that provide a relatively personal class setting.

Rolling Admissions – A form of admissions. Most commonly found at public institutions, schools with this type of policy continue to accept students throughout the year until their class sizes are met. For example, some schools begin accepting students as early as December and will continue to do so until April or May.

Room and Board – This figure is typically the combined cost of a university-owned room and a meal plan.

Room Draw/Housing Lottery – A common way to pick on-campus room assignments for the following year. If a student decides to remain in university-owned housing, he or she is assigned a unique number that, along with seniority, is used to determine his or her housing for the next year.

Rush – The period in which students can meet the brothers and sisters of a particular chapter and find out if a given fraternity or sorority is right for them. Rushing a fraternity or a sorority is not a requirement at any school. The goal of rush is to give students who are serious about pledging a feel for what to expect.

Semester System – The most common type of academic calendar system at college campuses. This setup typically includes two semesters in a given school year. The fall semester starts around the end of August or early September and concludes before winter vacation. The spring semester usually starts in mid-January and ends in late April or May.

Student Center/Rec Center/Student Union – A common area on campus that often contains study areas, recreation facilities, and eateries. This building is often a good place to meet up with fellow students; depending on the school, the student center can have a huge role or a non-existent role in campus life.

Student ID – A university-issued photo ID that serves as a student's key to school-related functions. Some schools require students to show these cards in order to get into dorms, libraries, cafeterias, and other facilities. In addition to storing meal plan information, in some cases, a student ID can actually work as a debit card and allow students to purchase things from bookstores or local shops.

Suite – A type of dorm room. Unlike dorms that feature communal bathrooms shared by the entire floor, suites offer bathrooms shared only among the suite. Suite-style dorm rooms can house anywhere from two to ten students.

TA (Teacher's Assistant) – An undergraduate or grad student who helps in some manner with a specific course. In some cases, a TA will teach a class, assist a professor, grade assignments, or conduct office hours.

Undergraduate – A student in the process of studying for his or her bachelor's degree.

About the Author

Name: Sana Khan

Hometown: Lauderhill, FL

Major: Biochemistry/Mathematics

Fun Fact: Sana has a black belt in tae kwon do!

Previous Contributors: Shawn Wines

Pros and Cons

Still can't figure out if this is the right school for you?
You've already read through this in-depth guide;
why not list the pros and cons? It will really help
with narrowing down your decision and determining
whether or not this school is right for you.

Pros	Cons
....	....
....	....
....	....
....	....
....	....
....	....
....	....
....	....
....	....
....	....
....	....
....	....

Pros and Cons

Still can't figure out if this is the right school for you?
You've already read through this in-depth guide;
why not list the pros and cons? It will really help
with narrowing down your decision and determining
whether or not this school is right for you.

Pros	**Cons**
....	....
....	....
....	....
....	....
....	....
....	....
....	....
....	....
....	....
....	....
....	....
....	....

Notes

....

....

....

....

....

....

....

....

....

....

....

....

....

....

....

Notes

....

....

....

....

....

....

....

....

....

....

....

....

....

....

....

Notes

....

....

....

....

....

....

....

....

....

....

....

....

....

....

....

Notes

....
....
....
....
....
....
....
....
....
....
....
....
....
....
....

Notes

....

....

....

....

....

....

....

....

....

....

....

....

....

....

Notes

....

....

....

....

....

....

....

....

....

....

....

....

....

....

Review Your School!

Let your voice be heard.

Every year, thousands of students take our online survey to share their opinions about campus life.

Now's your chance to help millions of high school students choose the right college for them.

Tell us what life is really like at your school by taking our online survey or even uploading your own photos and videos!

And as our thanks to you for participating in our survey, we'll enter you into a random drawing for our $1,000 Monthly Survey Scholarship!

For more information, check out
www.collegeprowler.com/survey

WWW.COLLEGEPROWLER.COM

Write For Us!

Express your opinion. Get published!

Interested in being a published author? College Prowler is always on the lookout for current college students across the country to write the guides for their schools.

The contributing author position is a unique opportunity for eager college students to bolster their résumés and portfolios, become published authors both online and in print, and gain tremendous exposure to millions of high school students nationwide.

For more details, visit
www.collegeprowler.com/careers

Albion College
Alfred University
Allegheny College
Alverno College
American Intercontinental
  University Online
American University
Amherst College
Arizona State University
Ashford University
The Art Institute of
  California – Orange
  County
Auburn University
Austin College
Babson College
Ball State University
Bard College
Barnard College
Barry University
Baruch College
Bates College
Bay Path College
Baylor University
Beloit College
Bentley University
Berea College
Binghamton University
Birmingham Southern
  College
Bob Jones University
Boston College
Boston University
Bowdoin College
Bradley University
Brandeis University
Brigham Young University
Brigham Young
  University – Idaho
Brown University
Bryant University
Bryn Mawr College
Bucknell University
Cal Poly Pomona
California College
  of the Arts
California Institute
  of Technology
California Polytechnic
  State University
California State University
  – Monterey Bay
California State University
  – Northridge
California State University
  – San Marcos
Carleton College
Carnegie Mellon University
Case Western Reserve
  University
Catawba College
Catholic University
  of America

Centenary College
  of Louisiana
Centre College
Chapman University
Chatham University
City College of New York
City College of
  San Francisco
Claflin University
Claremont McKenna
  College
Clark Atlanta University
Clark University
Clemson University
Cleveland State University
Colby College
Colgate University
College of Charleston
College of Mount
  Saint Vincent
College of Notre
  Dame of Maryland
College of the Holy Cross
College of William & Mary
College of Wooster
Colorado College
Columbia College Chicago
Columbia University
Concordia University
  – Wisconsin
Connecticut College
Contra Costa College
Cornell College
Cornell University
Creighton University
CUNY Lehman College
CUNY Queens College
CUNY Queensborough
  Community College
Dalton State College
Dartmouth College
Davidson College
De Anza College
Del Mar College
Denison University
DePaul University
DePauw University
Diablo Valley College
Dickinson College
Dordt College
Drexel University
Duke University
Duquesne University
Earlham College
East Carolina University
Eckerd College
El Paso Community
  College
Elon University
Emerson College
Emory University
Fashion Institute of Design
  & Merchandising

Fashion Institute of
  Technology
Ferris State University
Florida Atlantic University
Florida Southern College
Florida State University
Fordham University
Franklin & Marshall
  College
Franklin Pierce University
Frederick Community
  College
Freed-Hardeman
  University
Furman University
Gannon University
Geneva College
George Mason University
George Washington
  University
Georgetown University
Georgia Institute of
  Technology
Georgia Perimeter College
Georgia State University
Germanna Community
  College
Gettysburg College
Gonzaga University
Goucher College
Grinnell College
Grove City College
Guilford College
Gustavus Adolphus
  College
Hamilton College
Hampshire College
Hampton University
Hanover College
Harvard University
Harvey Mudd College
Hastings College
Haverford College
Hillsborough Community
  College
Hofstra University
Hollins University
Howard University
Hunter College (CUNY)
Idaho State University
Illinois State University
Illinois Wesleyan University
Indiana Univ.–Purdue Univ.
  Indianapolis (IUPUI)
Indiana University
Iowa State University
Ithaca College
Jackson State University
James Madison University
Johns Hopkins University
Juniata College
Kansas State University
Kaplan University

Kent State University
Kenyon College
La Roche College
Lafayette College
Lawrence University
Lehigh University
Lewis & Clark College
Linfield College
Los Angeles City College
Los Angeles Valley College
Louisiana College
Louisiana State University
Loyola College in
  Maryland
Loyola Marymount
  University
Loyola University Chicago
Luther College
Macalester College
Macomb Community
  College
Manhattan College
Manhattanville College
Marlboro College
Marquette University
Maryville University
Massachusetts College
  of Art & Design
Massachusetts Institute
  of Technology
McGill University
Merced College
Mercyhurst College
Messiah College
Miami University
Michigan State University
Middle Tennessee
  State University
Middlebury College
Millsaps College
Minnesota State
  University – Moorhead
Missouri State University
Montana State University
Montclair State University
Moorpark College
Mount Holyoke College
Muhlenberg College
New College of Florida
New York University
North Carolina A&T
  State University
North Carolina State
  University
Northeastern University
Northern Arizona
  University
Northern Illinois University
Northwest Florida
  State College
Northwestern College
  – Saint Paul
Northwestern University

Oakwood University
Oberlin College
Occidental College
Oglethorpe University
Ohio State University
Ohio University
Ohio Wesleyan University
Old Dominion University
Onondaga Community
College
Oral Roberts University
Pace University
Palm Beach State College
Penn State Altoona
Penn State Brandywine
Penn State University
Pepperdine University
Pitzer College
Pomona College
Princeton University
Providence College
Purdue University
Radford University
Ramapo College of
New Jersey
Reed College
Rensselaer Polytechnic
Institute
Rhode Island School
of Design
Rhodes College
Rice University
Rider University
Robert Morris University
Rochester Institute
of Technology
Rocky Mountain College
of Art & Design
Rollins College
Rowan University
Rutgers University
Sacramento State
Saint Francis University
Saint Joseph's University
Saint Leo University
Salem College
Salisbury University
Sam Houston State
University
Samford University
San Diego State University
San Francisco State
University
Santa Clara University
Santa Fe College
Sarah Lawrence College
Scripps College
Seattle University
Seton Hall University
Simmons College
Skidmore College
Slippery Rock University
Smith College

South Texas College
Southern Methodist
University
Southwestern University
Spelman College
St. John's College
– Annapolis
St. John's University
St. Louis University
St. Mary's University
St. Olaf College
Stanford University
State University of New
York – Purchase College
State University of New
York at Fredonia
State University of New
York at Oswego
Stetson University
Stevens-Henager College
Stony Brook University
(SUNY)
Susquehanna University
Swarthmore College
Syracuse University
Taylor University
Temple University
Tennessee State University
Texas A&M University
Texas Christian University
Texas Tech
The Community College
of Baltimore County
Towson University
Trinity College (Conn.)
Trinity University (Texas)
Troy University
Truman State University
Tufts University
Tulane University
Union College
University at Albany
(SUNY)
University at Buffalo
(SUNY)
University of Alabama
University of Arizona
University of Arkansas
University of Arkansas
at Little Rock
University of California
– Berkeley
University of
California – Davis
University of
California – Irvine
University of California
– Los Angeles
University of California
– Merced
University of California
– Riverside
University of California
– San Diego

University of California
– Santa Barbara
University of California
– Santa Cruz
University of Central
Florida
University of Chicago
University of Cincinnati
University of Colorado
University of Connecticut
University of Delaware
University of Denver
University of Florida
University of Georgia
University of Hartford
University of Illinois
University of Illinois
at Chicago
University of Iowa
University of Kansas
University of Kentucky
University of Louisville
University of Maine
University of Maryland
University of Maryland
– Baltimore County
University of
Massachusetts
University of Miami
University of Michigan
University of Minnesota
University of Mississippi
University of Missouri
University of Montana
University of Mount Union
University of Nebraska
University of Nevada
– Las Vegas
University of New
Hampshire
University of North
Carolina
University of North
Carolina – Greensboro
University of Notre Dame
University of Oklahoma
University of Oregon
University of Pennsylvania
University of Phoenix
University of Pittsburgh
University of Puget Sound
University of Rhode Island
University of Richmond
University of Rochester
University of San Diego
University of San Francisco
University of South
Carolina
University of South Dakota
University of South Florida
University of Southern
California
University of St
Thomas – Texas

University of Tampa
University of Tennessee
University of Tennessee
at Chattanooga
University of Texas
University of Utah
University of Vermont
University of Virginia
University of Washington
University of Western
Ontario
University of Wisconsin
University of
Wisconsin – Stout
Urbana University
Ursinus College
Valencia Community
College
Valparaiso University
Vanderbilt University
Vassar College
Villanova University
Virginia Commonwealth
University
Virginia Tech
Virginia Union University
Wagner College
Wake Forest University
Warren Wilson College
Washington &
Jefferson College
Washington & Lee
University
Washington University
in St. Louis
Wellesley College
Wesleyan University
West Los Angeles College
West Point Military
Academy
West Virginia University
Western Illinois University
Western Kentucky
University
Wheaton College (Ill.)
Wheaton College (Mass.)
Whitman College
Wilkes University
Willamette University
Williams College
Xavier University
Yale University
Youngstown State
University

CPSIA information can be obtained at www.ICGtesting.com
Printed in the USA
BVOW080204090812

297440BV00007B/2/P